D1014653

Perfume from Provence

Perfume from Provence

Lady Winifred Fortescue

Preface by Patricia Wells

Illustrated by

E. H. SHEPARD

Hearst Books
New York

TO

"MONSIEUR"

*"He is a portion of the loveliness
Which once he made more lovely"* . . .

Preface copyright © 1993 by Patricia Wells

First published in Great Britain in 1935 by William Blackwood & Sons Ltd.
Printed in Great Britian in 1992 by Transworld Publishers Ltd.

All rights reserved. No part of this book may be reproduced or utilized in any form
or by any means, electronic or mechanical, including photocopying, recording or
by any information storage or retrieval system, without permission in writing from
the Publisher. Inquiries should be addressed to Permissions Department, William
Morrow and Company, Inc., 1350 Avenue of the Americas, New York, N.Y. 10019.

It is the policy of William Morrow and Company, Inc., and its imprints and affiliates,
recognizing the importance of preserving what has been written, to print the books
we publish on acid-free paper, and we exert our best efforts to that end.

Library of Congress Cataloging-in-Publication Data

Fortescue, Winifred, Lady, b. 1888.
     Perfume from Provence / Lady Winifred Fortescue.
         p.   cm.
     1. Fortescue, Winifred, Lady, b. 1888—Homes and haunts—France—
   Provence.   2. Provence (France)—Social life and customs.
   3. British—France—Provence—Humor.   I. Title.
   DC611.P961F6   1993
   944'.9—dc20   92-39249
                                                                CIP

ISBN 0-688-12582-4

Printed in the United States of America

First U.S. Edition

   2 3 4 5 6 7 8 9 10

CONTENTS

PREFACE

Like many foreigners before them, and those yet to come, Lord and Lady Fortescue bought an old farmhouse in Provence and, in the bargain, found themselves starring in a real-life drama of southern French country life.

Their story is cast in the 1930s, when the titled English couple adopt a new culture, with no choice but to accept the assigned roles of the bourgeois, naive, gullible inexperienced *étranger*. Meanwhile, the French peasant (cast variously as mason/plumber/cleaning lady/gardener/auto mechanic) dutifully plays the part of the bumbling, devious, exasperating, and ever-predictable employee, friend, neighbor, and philosopher.

Caricatures? Only in part. And only as shadows of true-life individuals in a multicultural, multiclass drama. For each of us plays his or her character in a unique, specific way. And if the role is played with honesty, integrity, and a sense of humor, those who observe it come away culturally, philosophically, and emotionally enriched.

While there may be sixty years of distance between Lady Fortescue's experience and my own, as I read *Perfume from Provence,* I found myself nodding, laughing, and sighing with all too familiar recognition at her day-to-day foibles, frustrations, joys, and discoveries. Between the 1930s and the 1990s little of real substance has changed in Provence, despite the presence of fast-speed trains, McDonald's, rooftop satellite dishes, and next-day deliveries from Federal Express.

Daily life in Provence still tests our daily mettle as adopted foreigners, in a very big way. Life here brings us eyeball to eyeball with the very French culture we came to witness, experience, and share. It is more than sunshine that draws us to Provence: We come because life here seems more real, less modern, more slowly paced, more personal, and more richly human than almost any other place we know on earth. I don't think any of us comes expecting to become Provençal. But I suspect we do come to be part of a culture that does seem to stand very still. We love the juxtaposition of the old world and the new. We relish the rich, sometimes frustrating, often humorous contrast of cultures. When we get the mix just right, it brings about greater understanding and new respect for both worlds, with a whole treasure chest of mysteries still to be unraveled.

Lady Fortescue proves that you don't get to know a culture—or somehow find your place in it—by reading books, watching films, perfecting your accent, or mastering the use of the subjunctive. You get to know it by figuring out how to convince a gardener to grow pink, ivory, and pale lilac flowers when all he has ever known is sharp crimson, screaming orange, and deep purple. By laughing along with the plumber when he politely informs you that you must buy a bathtub deep enough to cover monsieur's belly. By pretending not to know that you are being swindled by the cleaning lady, the fishmonger, or the auto mechanic. By building a font of admiration and respect for a mason who seems to have been born knowing how to construct beautiful, sturdy walls of stones gathered willy-nilly from nearby fields; or for gardeners who can glance at the moon and know instinctively why this is the precise day to plant radishes that will thrive and why it is an equally disastrous time to prune the old cherry tree. And by allowing your personal life to become intertwined with theirs, and theirs with yours.

What is endearing about Lady Fortescue's account—and the reason to read it some sixty years later—is that her portrait of Provence is more than skin deep. She captures the characters and the culture in a simple, straightforward style, introducing us to those annoying merchants who resolutely refuse to sell you what you want; to an entire culture that lives for a crisis and thrives on catastrophe; to a land where plants are never purchased, but rather they are shared, or divided, grown from cuttings or sprout all on their own from the rocky, unforgiving soil. We nod in recognition when the village policeman comes to "inspect" the property, knowing all the while he really has an eye on the liquor cabinet and is confident of our generosity. We are reminded of the importance of the family ("which comes before the amassing of money"), and learn again that with patience, and just a little bit of humor, one can obtain all ones desires in Provence.

Lady Fortescue does not attempt to fit in, to become "one of them" and she has a great ability to laugh at herself and her own intransigent character. Along with her, we worry that our "stock of French adjectives" will give out all too quickly while attending a deeply boring, obligatory social occasion, and throw up our arms in utter frustration as we are confronted by yet another saint's day that manages to paralyze all commercial activity in our little village.

PREFACE

Although at times Lady Fortescue's superior, class-conscious tone appears outdated and out of place, her clear perception of daily life in Provence wins us over in the end. She proves that life in a country that is not our own helps us confront ourselves more directly, and encourages us to examine life in greater detail. And she reminds us that foreigners are perhaps the finest observers—and ambassadors—of any culture.

—PATRICIA WELLS
Provence, 1993

BUILDING.

"Madame! Madame! MADAME!"

A chorus of voices—French, Provençal, and Italian—all yelling for me at once. What could be the matter *now*?

I had grown accustomed to these howls for help during the many weeks in which our army of workmen had been enlarging the little golden house we had bought—before the £ collapsed—in Provence. Hardly a day passed without a visit from one or other of them : the electrician with a finger cut by wire ; a mason with a smashed thumb ; various *blessés* with casualties greater or less, all howling for ' Madame ' and tincture of iodine.

I hurried downstairs in the direction of the present howls, and found, outside the front door, a crowd of pale-faced workmen surrounding the prostrate form of a tall handsome boy who was lying in a pool of blood on the stone stairway leading to the terrace above.

At first I thought he had fallen from the scaffolding, and I felt sick with apprehension, but a few inquiries elicited the fact that it was merely a very bad nose hæmorrhage, and that the poor boy was subject to them. Of course, his *camarades* were, like workmen all the world over, paralysed by the sight of blood, and stood around gabbling excitedly but doing nothing. They turned on me, as one man, and informed me that *le pauvre malheureux* had lost at least two litres of good red blood in the tower before they could get him down.

With cold water applications I soon stopped the hæmorrhage, and after much coaxing persuaded him to enter my car and let me drive him to his home. He was terrified lest he might soil the new cushions, and only when enveloped in a bath-towel would he consent to get in.

All his comrades, of course, rushed to open the gate, falling over each other, shouting encouragement to the invalid and waving us farewell with every variety of gaudy coloured handkerchief. I knew that after our departure all work would remain in abeyance while *le pauvre malheureux* was discussed, and that not until they had comfortably interred him in imagination, with suitable *pompe funèbre*, would it be resumed.

I had grown to love these excitable emotional men of the South and to regard them as my children—for they were little more. They were perfectly maddening, entirely without initiative, and quite irresponsible, but they were most lovable. And I wonder what woman could resist the unconscious way an Italian peasant makes love to her with his eyes while he is taking her orders ?

For I found that I had to give orders. In Provence it is always Madame who conducts all business. In England the Contractor does everything, but we learned early that in Provence the *Entrepreneur* is only responsible for his masonry and his masons. It was my pleasing job to find carpenter, painter, plumber, electrician, and ironworker, and, after that, to make these men work together.

The old bald-headed *Entrepreneur* was splendid at his job, having grown old in his profession. He supplied the practical suggestions, and, being an Italian with a great artistic sense, he understood at once my love of line and of dignified simplicity and my passion for the apsidal ending and the Provençal arch. So we dispensed with the services of an architect and got on famously together. When I asked if such and such a thing were possible, he would stand silent for a while, his old bald head bent in thought and a gnarled forefinger curled round his nose. Then, the problem solved in his fertile brain, he would shoot up his head, his black eyes twinkling under shaggy brows, throw up his hands to Heaven and exclaim, " *Mais—DIABLE ! OUI, Madame !* " and waddle off to instruct his masons, enthusiastic as a boy.

He was childishly pleased with praise of his men's work, though they never got a word of it from him. His old eyes would fill with tears when I told him that not one fruit or flower had been taken from our garden ; or when I described the beautiful courtesy of his workmen who rushed to help me in every conceivable way, seizing baskets and bundles from my arms to carry them for me, and standing cap in hand in the hot sun when I spoke to them until I begged them " *Couvrez-vous, je vous prie.*" Yet he seemed to spend his life in scolding and driving them whenever he appeared. His masons seldom obeyed him silently. Generally they argued with him for a quarter of an hour before they went off, grumbling, to the tasks he set them. But although he always got his way in the end, he could not make his men work harmoniously with the craftsmen of other professions. That was Madame's task, and to accomplish it she had to be among the workmen all day and every day.

My knowledge of technical French was *nil* when the building operations began, but I found my natural gift for dancing more valuable than anything else. If one only danced energetically

4

enough, things got done, and, with violent gesture and childish drawings, I managed to convey my wishes and ideas. Once I had won the men's hearts—so easily done with a joke, a compliment,

" Scolding and driving them whenever he appeared."

and little acts of consideration for their welfare— I found that the word *blessée* did all the rest. If Madame were ' wounded ' about something left undone that ought to have been done, that thing was immediately accomplished. If she appeared,

grave-eyed and sorrowful, in the midst of some
noisy childish dispute, the tumult and the shouting
died.

And so I did somehow contrive to make the
men work together, not always harmoniously, for
to mix Italians and French is to attempt to mix
oil and water. The result was always noisy and
generally exciting. The men chattered and
squabbled furiously as they performed miracles
of terrifying agility upon scaffolding, but they
would break off abruptly in the midst of a ferocious
argument to gaze together in silence at some
lovely effect of light upon a mountain, all acrimony
forgotten, united for a few seconds in their love
of the beautiful. Then, as suddenly, they would
return to the battle with Southern intensity.

One such argument nearly deafened us one
morning. We were having our *petit déjeuner* in
our little *salon* when a startling flood of noisy
eloquence washed us to our feet. Outside the
east window were gathered the foreman, the head-
painter, the electrician, and the carpenter, wrang-
ling about a patch of damp which had stained
the inside wall below the window. Whose fault
was this ? None of theirs, it seemed.

The foreman, his face distorted, puce in colour,
whined and shrilled in an Italian falsetto as he
defended his masons. The head-painter, a dear

6

fat old Provençal, his rotund form clad in white paint-smirched overalls and his pink cherubic face crowned by a ridiculous tall paper hat made from a pilfered copy of ' The Times,' shouted in an olive-oily baritone and bounced about like an indiarubber ball, his blue eyes flashing with the excitement of debate. The electrician, a voluble Parisian, emphasised his points with jerky gestures and expressed his innocence in torrents of clipped French in a high tenor voice, while the carpenter, a beautiful, blue-eyed, black-haired giant of twenty-three, drowned the other three combatants with his great bubbling bass. Their arms whirled in the air like flails.

Just as I was wondering wearily whether I must leave my fragrant coffee and once again intervene —this time *en peignoir*—the battle ceased as suddenly as it had begun, and the belligerent quartette dispersed laughing merrily.

They had decided to wait for *le bon Dieu* to send another rainfall ; and then, if the stain got larger, they would decide whether it were masonry, paint-work, wiring, or carpentry that was at fault. Typical of Provence where every problem will be solved and every plea answered " *Demain, ou après-demain* " (and it is generally *après-demain*).

So we were left in peace—with our stained wall —to finish our interrupted breakfast.

We had signed our contract in June, but the building operations were not begun until after our arrival in September, for the Provençaux are terrified of responsibility. As the house is built on the slope of a mountain and the garden is terraced, it was necessary to dig very deep for the foundations of the new rooms, and naturally, therefore, we were overtaken by bad weather. November is the month when Provence relies upon the heavens for its annual water-supply, and certainly it got more than its full measure in 1931. As all work ceases in this country when it is wet, and everyone goes to ground the moment the first drop of rain descends, our building got badly delayed. With despairing eyes we watched our workmen bolting for home under huge umbrellas with the first shower. Even Hilaire, our old gardener, would rush under cover and chop wood, muffled to the eyes, only emerging cautiously under his gigantic gamp to cross five yards of open ground when the time came to feed the rabbits.

Then later came the hardest winter known in Provence for years—fourteen degrees of frost up in our mountains (1100 to 1200 feet above the sea), and my little cascade in the rose-garden hung with icicles eighteen inches long. Again the masons could not work. Used to hot sunshine in winter, they shivered in their thin overalls. The oldest of them all, whom I called '*Monsieur le Chef*,' because when he was not stirring his eternal puddings of mortar outside our front door he was heating up the tin mugs of vegetable soup for his fellow-workmen, still strove to mix his cement with water which froze as he mixed. He looked so pitifully frail and thin, his creaky laugh wheezing faintly as he tried to hearten his congealed companions, that I wrapped him from head to toe in a heavy peasant's cloak. In this he still laboured valiantly, looking like a very ancient hooded crow.

"*Muffled to the eyes . . . to feed the rabbits.*"

But always, after half an hour's effort, we heard the foreman's ominous 'cease work' whistle, and the whole army of workmen would drift off, gibbering with cold and blowing upon their frozen hands. Even their vocal chords seemed to be affected by frost and the eternal stream of chatter to be frozen in their throats. They trudged and shuffled silently away. . . . More delay—then—snow !

From our windows we looked out upon an enchanted land. The grey waves of olive foliage which surge and billow over valleys and mountains to the blue Mediterranean were powdered with fine snow and sparkled under an azure sky. Here and there tall cypresses, planted in pairs near each old Provençal homestead, one for *La Paix* and one for *La Prospérité*, stood out like black pointed rocks in the glittering sea. On the old golden-grey terrace walls and stairways late pink roses and pansy faces peeped through the snow, and even the hideous heaps of excavated earth in our garden were transformed into miniature ranges of snow-mountains.

Our little merry - eyed Italian *bonne*, Emilia, spent most of her time rushing out-of-doors to pick up handfuls of snow, toss it in the air, taste it, and press it into snowballs, which she was much too polite to throw at the workmen. "*Madame! la neige! la belle neige! Regardez les oliviers qu'ils sont beaux sous la neige!*" A new and thrilling phenomenon for her, coming as she does from the hot sunshine of Southern Italy.

It was all very pretty and amusing to watch, but the housework suffered, the garden suffered, and our poor building operations suffered.

The old *Entrepreneur* had promised us that all should be finished by December 20th, 1931, and I, rashly believing him, gave him a month's margin and ordered our furniture and possessions, stored in London till the house should be ready to receive them, to be sent over in mid-January. Time was slipping on, and not even my husband's long gallery on the ground floor was finished yet. The unusual weather provided an excellent excuse for the delay in the building, and we were getting desperate.

" *Madame ! la neige !* "

However, at last came the blessed thaw, and once more the work progressed, though slowly still. No doubtful point could be decided under half an hour, because it appeared to be essential and usual for every expert of each separate trade to down tools and rush to the debate whatever it might be. Each man had, of course, entirely different views, which he defended with vigour and violence, and, as it always fell to Madame to make the final decision, she found that building in Provence was anxious work. However, it was only necessary to make the men laugh and all was well.

Consideration for our comfort was genuinely the chief object of them all, though their opinions as to how this was to be assured might differ. When it came to the choosing of fittings for our bathroom, the head-plumber was most urgent that the bath should be deep enough so that the water should cover ' *l'estomac de Monsieur* ' (such a little one, too), and that a certain useful seat should be of good mahogany and " *bien arrondi pour le confort de Madame,*" who fled on the excuse that she heard a phantom telephone bell.

And so at last we had at any rate a bathroom actually finished, though its completion was delayed, as usual, by rain. When the fittings did not appear on the day appointed for their arrival, I telephoned to the plumber to inquire the cause. He replied that he could not possibly risk damage to the beautiful *appareil* in such weather. (Damage to a *bath*, a *basin*, &c., by WATER !) The fittings would be sent " *demain, ou après-demain.*" Of course they would.

Although the continued delays were very expensive and caused us great anxiety and much irritation of spirit, still I loved watching the men at their tasks. There was Big Jean, a huge dour-faced mason, who shovelled stones from the foundations and threw them into a narrow wooden trough fourteen feet above his head without ever dropping one. When I spoke admiringly of his skill to Emilia, she at once gave me every detail of his life-story, and I learned that each day he had to leave an invalid wife, whom he adored, alone and in bed, for he must earn bread for them both. That evening I picked a gay bouquet of flowers and slipped it into his great hands to cheer her sad solitude. To my consternation the granite face broke up and two big tears rolled down his dusty cheeks. From that moment he became my very devoted slave, competing with *Monsieur le Chef* for the first daily hand-shake.

The hand-shaking in Provence is most exhausting. My hand was shaken at least sixty times a day, shaken in greeting, in parting, and on every possible pretext, by every variety of hand in every possible condition of dirt. The old veteran, posing black-and-white tiles in the hall like a jig-saw puzzle, would pause in his work to shake hands ; the foreman, plastering huge boulders over an overflow pipe so that the water should burst through the perforated stones in a series of tiny cascades in my rose-garden, would proffer a slimy hand directly I appeared. Another artist, building up the big arched Provençal open fireplace of narrow rose-coloured bricks in the gallery, dropped his trowel so to salute me ; and the phlegmatic-looking mason hollowing out a niche over the door in my little blue *salon* to hold a tiny Madonna, bent from his ladder with paw outstretched. And so it went on all day. We kept a supply of pumice - stone, turpentine, and patent cleansers ever ready in the bathroom to remove the traces of our workmen's warmth of heart and hand.

We grew very fond of them all, and the trouble was that they returned our affection and were therefore unwilling to put an end to a pleasant experience. Love was being mixed with the mortar, we knew, but love can be leisurely, and at last I had to dance more and more energetically to hustle the old *Entrepreneur*.

After that, *camions* (lorries) came thick and fast, crashing down our little approach, slicing Hilaire's cherished grass, damaging his neat drive and discharging their loads of gravel and lime in a cloud of choking dust. Planks and boards arrived in a cart drawn by a vicious mule, who employed the time of unloading by kicking up the paths and munching Hilaire's precious pansies. My life was further complicated by the need of pacifying a frantic gardener.

Hilaire did not love the workmen. To him the old *Entrepreneur* was the archdemon and his horde of masons a legion of devils who trampled upon his choice plants, broke off branches from his fruit-trees, and covered his vines with clouds of cement dust. Above all, he hated *Monsieur le Chef*. He it was who smothered the scarlet geraniums with lime, who sullied the clear water of the little fountain when cleaning his horrible shovel, who scorched the finest peach-tree on the lower terrace by making his little hell of lighted olive twigs and fir cones just beneath it to perform his cooking operations. Between Hilaire and *Monsieur le Chef* raged constant war, and, in spite of his eighty-four years and his toothlessness, it was amazing to hear the cataract of sarcastic retaliation the old mason poured over Hilaire's furious protests. I had rather a special weakness for the gallant old man, and once he even made mischief on this score between Hilaire and me, saying that Madame never scolded him, Madame always shook him by the hand first of all, and so on. On that occasion it was quite difficult to make my peace.

No accident nor misfortune that happened to any one of the workmen drew the slightest sympathy from Hilaire. It was either the man's own silly fault, or a just visitation from *le bon Dieu*, or else a case of malingering. When I inquired after the welfare of my poor young mason who had the severe nasal hæmorrhage, to my amazement

Hilaire only grinned, tapped his old nose significantly and assured me, " *Ce n'est rien, Madame, ce n'est rien !* " And when I indignantly protested that the poor boy had had a very serious hæmorrhage, Hilaire replied knowingly, " *Jeune marié ! Jeune marié ! Il faut aller doucement ! Il faut aller doucement !* "

When Hilaire becomes Rabelaisian I am fain to flee.

I had been warned by a resident that when the roof went on to the little Provençal tower which surmounts the new building, *La Cabade* would be celebrated, and we should be lucky if there was a flower or a branch left in our garden. The workmen, I was told, would decorate their work and expect a half-holiday and bottles of wine to drink to the health of the house. What would happen with Hilaire then ? I foresaw that unless I could prevail upon him to drink at least three bottles of wine, this feast was likely to become a second Passover and our lintel splashed with blood.

I begged the old *Entrepreneur* to give me fair warning when this celebration would take place, and asked how I should know when to buy my wine and make my preparations. He only put his old hands on his thighs, bent his knees and laughed soundlessly at some secret joke of his own. Then, when I pressed for an answer, he looked at me with twinkling eyes and wagging head, and assured me that I could not possibly miss it when the moment came.

But when *would* that moment come ? we wondered apprehensively. Our furniture was due to arrive in less than a month, and so far no room was ready to receive it. The *Entrepreneur* swore that at any rate he would have the old part of the house habitable by then, and we hoped that the long gallery in the new building would be completed also, because that was large enough to store all the surplus furniture for the new rooms.

But when the dread day came and we got a telephone message to say that the two vans of furniture had arrived at Nice and would be transported to us that day, the gallery was ceiled but not floored, and the bedrooms above were floored but not ceiled ! How were we to fit all our mass of stuff into a tiny hall, a diminutive *salon* and four wee bedrooms, which was all the accommodation that the old part of the house contained ?

We left the flat where we were living during the building operations and started for our mountain, two kilometres away, with heavy hearts. It was a bitterly cold day and freezing hard, but having no garage ready we were obliged to leave our new car in the only place wide enough for two cars to pass in the lane leading to our house— a rocky ravine near a waterfall. Not the ideal place in which to leave a new car with a stiff engine on a wintry day, but we had no choice. Would she ever start again at night ? For our agonies would not abate till darkness fell, of that I felt sure. However—sufficient unto the day— and that day we had more than enough to worry about. So we muffled the bonnet with rugs and went ahead on foot.

Suddenly we both stopped simultaneously and looked at each other with a wild surmise as a roar as of many waters in spate met our ears. The first van ! It could be nothing else.

We hurried on in the direction of the roar, which suddenly ceased and was succeeded by mixed noises resembling those in a menagerie at feeding-time. As we drew nearer I distinguished a babel of voices, the minor howl of the Provençal peasant, the nasal Niçois twang, the bass bubbling of agitated Italians and the shrill exclamations of the French. Something had gone wrong. What could it be ?

We rounded a bend in the lane and came upon —the van ! There it stood in all its awful majesty, a Leviathan among vans, the most gigantic thing on wheels that I had ever seen. Round it surged a mixed mob of peasants and removal-men all pointing skywards and all yelling at once.

And then I realised the cause of the hubbub. A huge olive branch barred the way of this Monster of Transport invading the lovely peace of the mountains. I sympathised deeply with the protest of the old olive-tree—but I wanted my furniture. So I hurried forward to the scene of inaction.

Hilaire—of course Hilaire was in the centre of the crowd—saw me coming and rushed forward to give the first explanation, which was so painfully obvious, and the Niçois removal-men all turned upon me indignantly as though I had placed the bough there on purpose to obstruct their work. I ignored them, and suggested to Hilaire that the branch should be cut off. His eyes goggled, his mouth dropped open, and to his shocked protest was added a chorus of dissent from the crowd of collected peasants.

Cut off the branch of a sacred olive-tree ! A fine branch laden with fruit ? Of course, Madame was English and new to Provence, and had evidently not yet had time to learn that the olives were precious to the peasant.

I cut all this short by ordering Hilaire to go and find the proprietor of the olive yard and get his permission, offering to pay him compensation for the damage to his tree.

The Monster of Transport.

Hilaire lumbered off down the mountain leaving us to be lectured by the excited crowd. He returned after a short time to inform us that it was a *fête* day and the owner of the tree was not at home. *Impasse*. More conversation. And then suddenly Monsieur, generally a very patient man, grew desperate. Eyeglass fixed in a very fierce eye, he strode into the midst of the group, and towering over the men commanded that the branch should be cut off AT ONCE.

" Get a saw," ordered Monsieur curtly, turning upon Hilaire, who fled towards the house to do his bidding, returning with many saws, ropes, and tackle.

Then a discussion arose as to who should cut off the branch ; and suddenly they all became as eager to cut it off as they had been anxious to save it. Fourteen men rushed at the tree and began scrambling up it, shouting and squabbling as they climbed.

At this juncture we decided to crawl round or under the van and go on to the house, there to prepare for the arrival of the Monster which presumably would be freed in an hour's time.

After two hours the tractor appeared round the bend of the lane dragging the enormous van, and, at this thrilling sight, every workman in the building hurled down his tools and rushed to the edge of the scaffolding platforms to watch its arrival. Cries of

" *Mon Dieu !* "

" *Diable !* "

" *Sapristi !* "

" *Sacré nom d'un nom !* "

" *Quel horreur !* "

" *Madonna mia !* "

rent the air, and Emilia tied on a huge apron and began rolling up her sleeves, murmuring " *Dieu d'Amour !* " with sparkling eyes.

For though she thoroughly enjoyed a crisis, she positively loved a catastrophe; and when the van, released from its tractor, rushed down to the front door by its own momentum and leaned wearily against the porch, thereby completely blocking the main entrance to the house, it looked very like a catastrophe. The united efforts of the removal-men assisted by the whole army of our workmen (delighted to do any other work than their own) failed to move it; and there we were, stuck once more. The only alternative was to unload the van and carry its contents up two stone stairways to another entrance on the terrace above.

The Niçois, tired and furious, of course protested violently, but we were firm. Enough time had been wasted, and the second van was yet to come. I reminded them of this, and was informed, consolingly, that the second van contained all the *heavy* furniture, and that ' The Son of a Pig ' could not start till the tractor went back to fetch it. That, anyhow, was some small comfort. I felt that I could perhaps cope with one pig at a time.

We found that the Nice firm only undertook to dump our goods at their destination, and, as they insisted upon taking with them all empty crates and packing materials, we must unpack every single one of the gigantic cases of crockery and glass ourselves.

Well, somehow my husband and I accomplished this tremendous task, aided only by Hilaire and Emilia, who had evidently never enjoyed an experience so much in their lives. The unpacking was somewhat delayed because they wanted to examine, stroke, and praise all *les belles choses* as they emerged from their wrappings.

At intervals I rushed out-of-doors to instruct the removal-men as to where things were to be dumped. To do them justice they worked with fury once they had begun, though with ill-will. They ought to have been very grateful for all the voluntary assistance given to them by the masons, plumbers, painters, electricians, and iron-workers who had permanently deserted their own work to join in the fun—but nothing seemed to please them.

At length the first van was actually depleted, the empty cases packed into it, the tractor attached once more, and the horrible Monster thundered off down the drive. The struggle was over for a time; *Monsieur le Chef* appeared with his mugs of onion soup, and the workmen all squatted down among the shavings and *débris* to discuss the exciting events of the morning. For our part, we sank exhausted upon a few stray cushions and ate our sandwiches in apprehensive silence, knowing that ' The Son of a Pig ' would soon be grunting on his way from Nice.

" What a morning ! " exclaimed Madame.

" With a hell of an afternoon ahead ! " ejaculated Monsieur.

And the little *bonne*, looking from one to the other with dancing eyes, suddenly banged down the coffee she had contrived to make amid the wreckage in the kitchen, held her little fat sides, and laughed and laughed and laughed.

" *Dieu d'Amour !* " she gasped when she could speak. After which we all felt better.

Our coffee was interrupted by a deputation of enraged men. The second van had, it appeared, arrived, but was sunk in our mountain lane half a kilometre away from the house. The ' Son of a Pig ' had, we were informed, crushed a wall, and was in danger of rushing down the mountain like his Gaderene ancestors. Of course, it was *our* fault, as had been the mishap of the morning.

Only the mad English would send such fantastic vans to climb the mountains of France, to spoil the valuable olive-trees and crush walls laboriously made by the poor peasants. Now, the Niçois supposed, we should expect *them* to unload the van in the lane and carry huge masses of heavy furniture to the house—work for giants and not for mere men whose families relied upon them for bread. If we insisted upon such work we might have murder upon our souls, and widows and fatherless children upon our consciences for the rest of our mortal lives.

The workmen, roused from their slumbers by the arrival of the men, had risen from their curious recumbent attitudes, heads on buckets, legs curled round a branch, and were listening intently. Big Jean suggested scornfully that a jack might be found and the van levered out of the road. Various masons volunteered to prop up the falling wall, " *Diable! ce n'etait rien!* " And the whole band of them, enchanted once more to leave their own jobs and join in the fray, hustled off the Niçois to the scene of the disaster.

The van was eventually levered out and the wall shored up, and then the tractor dragging the huge van came crashing down the mountain, rushed through our entrance, carrying away a gatepost, slicing once more Hilaire's precious grass, and smashing a young cherry-tree; and the two, van and tractor, locked together by the force of impact, came to rest near our garage.

Slumbering attitude.

Then, of course, they had to be disentangled and dismantled before the doors of the van could be opened. However, with forty people assisting, this did not take very long, and soon the work proceeded.

Working with sulky removal-men, who obviously held us responsible for every difficulty that had to be surmounted, was not very heartening. But suddenly a very little thing changed their whole attitude. The first object to be unpacked from the second van was a gnarled oak root, transformed into a thing of beauty by the artist who fashioned the Elfin Oak in Kensington Gardens for the children of London. As I unwrapped it and the Niçois beheld the forms of fairies, gnomes, pixies, lizards, mice, an owl, a frog, and a rat, found in the natural contortions of the wood, moulded further and then painted, they grouped around me silent and fascinated. English workmen would have picked up the root and dumped it in a room with other junk, unremarked. Not so these impressionable Southerners.

Seizing my opportunity I told them the story of the wonderful Elfin Oak of Kensington Gardens, describing the seventy-five figures of birds, beasts, and The Little People the artist had found in it. The men listened enthralled ; they had naturally never seen anything like it before. They stroked the little beasts with grimy forefingers and noticed their gleaming eyes.

My husband grew impatient, not realising the

importance of the incident, but I finished my story, and then, with great sighs as though waking from a dream, they walked back to the van. But the fairies had bewitched them with their magic and transformed them from surly brutes into laughing, willing workers. They heaved heavy furniture on to their heads, and, puny as they looked, carried huge objects up steep terraces and stairways until, as dusk fell, the second van was empty and lumbered away. The battle was over, silence fell over the little domaine, and only the battlefield strewn with shavings and old newspapers told the tale of our struggles.

There was as yet no electric light in the house and we had no candles. It was impossible to sleep in the house that night, so we decided to instal Hilaire as guardian. We fixed up a mattress on the floor, and I found three satin eiderdowns and a brocade cushion for his old bald head ; and there he lay with his double-barrelled fowling-piece beside him, unable to sleep for fear that *voleurs* would come, murder him first, and then make off with all *les belles choses* of Monsieur and Madame. So he told us next day, and I had reached the stage when I really wished they *had*, so gigantic seemed the task of getting the house into order.

For, at the end of the day, having no more room

to store anything indoors, out-houses being stacked from floor to ceiling, we had been driven in desperation to use the empty dog-kennels, hen-runs, and rabbit-houses. These were now filled with odd objects of all sorts which must be sorted and placed elsewhere.

The very last straw which finally broke our patient backs was when, worn out with fatigue, we discovered that our car would not start. We tried everything, but the oil in the engine seemed to have frozen hard. Wrapped in rugs we wandered up and down in the darkness while our little *bonne*, who knew the locality, went in search of a house with a telephone on which she could summon aid from a garage.

After an Arctic interval, succour came; the engine was made to work and we all drove back to the flat. So ended one of the most terrific days of our lives.

In two more we were actually installed in part of our house, where we lived in a cloud of cement dust to the accompaniment of the music of masons and carpenters for many exhausting weeks. The work began to go on more quickly after our installation, and one morning, on going out into the garden, I was startled to see the new building decorated with a mass of flags of all nations, the English predominating; branches of trees were tied to the scaffolding; bosses of ivy hung from poles; two little pine-trees adorned with huge bows of flame-coloured ribbon (a gift, as I afterwards learned, from the old *Entrepreneur* himself) flanked the entrance to the Gallery, and a complete pine-tree was lashed to the spike of the Provençal tower.

La Cabade was upon us! The roof was ON! Then I knew what was expected of us. Workmen's eager faces beamed at me from every hole in the building, and I climbed up and shook them each and all by the hand and thanked them for their lovely decorations.

My husband and I unearthed some blue curtains with which we decorated the inside of the garage, and rigged up a long trestle table. This I covered with blue cloths and decorated with bowls of violets, vases of carnations, and every cut-glass tumbler and wine-glass that I could find. We threw down blue garden cushions on plank benches, and then I drove down to the town and came back laden with bottles of red wine, tins of 'fancy' biscuits which I arranged in little silver cardboard shells on my table, packets of cigarettes and tobacco, and those wicked-looking slim black cheroots, beloved of all Italian workmen.

I put on a red chiffon frock with red shoes,

tucked red carnations in my hair (to look
Carnivalish), and went downstairs to receive my
guests.

I turned on a gay waltz on the gramophone,
and then my husband had an inspiration. He
blew a loud blast on our puppy-whistle in imitation
of the 'cease work' signal which had sounded
so often and sometimes so ominously in our ears.
The foreman's indignant face instantly peered
out of a window to see who was usurping his
authority, but when he saw my husband twinkling
at him from below, he rocked with laughter and
came scrambling down the scaffolding followed
by his thirty masons, who burst from every aperture
chattering and laughing like a crowd of excited
children.

We shook each by the hand (once more) and
led them to the garage. The old *Entrepreneur*
resplendent in his best broadcloth had arrived with
his chauffeur son, and he had the tact to invite
Hilaire to sit in the place of honour on his right
hand. Then Monsieur and Madame poured out
wine, proposed toasts, listened to good wishes,
and served out biscuits and cigars for two solid
hours. Everyone got very flushed; everyone
talked and laughed at once; everyone (except
the host and hostess) sang a solo, and all enjoyed
themselves hugely.

And, nicest of all, everyone helped to take down the curtains and to carry cushions, wine-glasses, &c., into the house after the feast before they all drove off in a *camion*, singing into the night.

But the great moment of my day came when I gave the giant carpenter his tip in an envelope (for everyone gets a tip in an envelope at parting on these occasions). He and I happened to be alone with Monsieur in the *salon* when I gave it, and, to our immense astonishment (and my delight), he bent his beautiful head and very reverently kissed me on both cheeks, murmuring his thanks as though he were singing under water.

My enjoyment would have been greater had my mind not been clouded by apprehension lest all the other workmen should salute me in like manner, none of them very clean and all very prickly with a week's growth of beard (*La Cabade* fell on a Saturday), but happily only my beautiful clean-shaven giant did me that honour.

It was wonderful to know that the roof was really ON, and that soon our army of workmen would depart. We should miss them in more ways than one, but we longed for peace and privacy. But at last they did leave us, shaking our hands in a frenzy of leave-taking, walking backwards down the drive waving their tools and shouting sad farewells till they were out of sight.

And now our little domaine is bathed in a beautiful peace, broken only by the sound of hidden mountain streams, an occasional crash of fallen crockery in the kitchen, and the frequent wail of Hilaire for " MADAME-E-E-E-e-e-e ! ! ! "

HILAIRE is tending his vines to-day. For months he has been alternately spraying the fruit with powdered sulphur and the leaves with *sulfate de cuivre* to keep off *la maladie* which, owing to the unwonted rain this summer, has attacked the vines in the valleys. Ours have escaped, all but a scorching here and there from the unprecedented August heat, and now Hilaire is tenderly tucking great bunches of white Muscats into net-bags to protect them from what he calls *méchantes abeilles* —which I call wasps.

A disastrous year for the crops of Provence, for the Clerk of the Weather has gone mad and has sent us everything out of season. But, as my fat peasant neighbour, Monsieur Pierre, remarks, what else can you expect this year, the anniversary in date and day, according to the Roman Catholic Calendar, of the murder of Our Lord ? Was not the President—*un brave homme*— assassinated ? Are there not floods, earthquakes, and other disasters all over the world ? *Que voulez-vous ?* Certainly no more of this extraordinary weather !

Even now, as Hilaire embags his grapes, lightning is tearing the clouds into jagged strips and thunder crashes overhead. In a moment rain will fall, and then, with the first drop, Hilaire will go to ground. He hides himself under the garage which projects over the lower terrace. Here he can chop up olive branches to add to the winter store, and talk to the rabbits in their yard close by at the same time; and here I often find him for a gossip.

"*Voilà le Directeur*," he says to me, pointing to our old chinchilla buck rabbit, whom he has separated from the lady rabbit and her newborn family of eight, " *Bon travailleur ! Maintenant—un peu de repos*," and Hilaire taps his old nose significantly. He is about to become Rabelaisian, and I hastily change the subject to vegetables, which seem safer. I tell him that Monsieur is fond of *courgettes* (things like little round or oval vegetable marrows) and that I want a lot of them sown.

Does Madame want melons as well? asks Hilaire with seeming irrelevance. Of course she does! What sane woman would not want the miracle of melons growing daily in the open air of her garden ? Then the melons must be planted at least one *hectare* away from the *courgettes* so that they cannot see each other, affirms Hilaire. " *Si non, ils se marient*," explains Hilaire to a mystified Madame (this sex question cropping up again), and the melons will become *courgettes*. Why do not *courgettes* become melons ? laments Madame. But it appears that in Nature with mixed alliances the plebeian type usually triumphs.

The rain has by this time ceased ; there has not been enough to soak the soil sufficiently, and I see my evening clearly outlined before me. Hilaire fixes me with a firm eye and asks if he shall attach the hose for Madame, as everything in the garden wants watering. Madame sighs resignedly. In ten minutes she will be wound in the beastly embrace of a 30-metre hose and cursing in its coils for the next two hours. And she had made such lovely plans to weed her precious rock-garden all by herself.

Monsieur, more wary, tiptoes forth from the *salon* door with a determined expression upon his face. Instantly he is hailed by Hilaire, who has already decided what work Monsieur shall do in the garden, for he values my husband's patient labour ; " *Monsieur travaille avec conscience !* " he allows. But Monsieur has his own ideas to-night, so pursues his way without turning his head. " *Le pauvre Monsieur est un peu sourd,*" murmurs Hilaire to me compassionately, and gives up the attempt to employ him this evening. Monsieur, not so deaf as Hilaire thinks, proceeds on his way,

carrying his beloved Dutch hoe, brought with him
from England, to dig up weeds in a remote corner
of the garden. As he passes me, poor weak slave
that I am, wound up in the hose and watering
myself almost as copiously as the garden, do I,

or do I not, de-
tect a triumphant
twinkle in his eye?
Now if Emilia had
set Monsieur a
task he would
slavishly have per-
formed it. The
sex question once
more.

I think Hilaire
finds watering with
the hose a boring
affair, and I cor-
dially agree with
him — it is. He

*" Irrigates the garden in the old primitive
way."*

has all the fun when he irrigates the garden in
the old primitive way. In Portugal water is
spilled upon the ground and the gardeners direct
it in the way it should go by standing in it and
wiggling their toes until little channels are made
in the mud. Here in Provence we are more
sophisticated. We make channels of cement,

connected with the great stone water-tank above on the highest terrace, and then release the water. Hilaire loves doing this. He rushes up the stone stairways to the *bassin*, big enough for a swimming bath, takes out a huge plug, and in a minute a glorious torrent of water comes cascading and gurgling down the cement channels which border the vegetable beds on every terrace.

" *La rivière, Madame !* " shouts Hilaire joyously as he thunders down the steps from terrace to terrace in his heavy peasant boots in pursuit of the rushing water. It overflows its banks and floods down the shallow trenches dug for this purpose between lines of tomatoes, *salades*, and every kind of vegetable. When each channel is a miniature stream, Hilaire feverishly rakes the soil at its end into a little dam to close it, while the water permeates gently to the roots of the plants. It is a thrilling game, as he has to be very quick ; for the volume of water is great, and as each trench fills and is dammed up, the main torrent rushes swiftly on and, if not directed into the prepared channels, would flood the terraces and endanger the walls. Water in a mountain country can be dangerous, and our little golden house is built on the side of a mountain and the garden is therefore terraced. I saw a rainstorm demolish a wall in November. Hilaire had just

warned me not to continue planting anemones
on a certain terrace because the wall was unsafe,
when, with a gentle rumbling sound, the wall
crumbled before our eyes, and an avalanche of
earth and boulders—and anemone roots—rolled
down into my rose garden on the terrace below.
My cherished rose garden which Hilaire, my
husband, and I had made with such labour only
a month before, and planted with lovely English
roses !

I shall never forget that funny planting !
Hilaire appeared paralysed when the great bales
of rose-trees arrived in a lorry from the station
and had to be layered in. He knew that Madame
had arranged a colour scheme, but he, though
he is unaware of the fact, is colour blind. I proved
this early when trying to explain to him that I
liked flowers of one colour massed together, or a
scheme of one or two delicate shades such as
mauve, pink, and white mingled. He had planted
a line of scarlet geraniums fronted with magenta
antirrhinums and orange marigolds, to surprise us
on our arrival. It did. . . .

When I explained my theory of planting he
said *now* he understood perfectly the wishes of
Madame. Plucking a scarlet geranium he held
it on high and bawled triumphantly " *Rose !* "
then, picking a pink stock, he shouted " *Mauve !* "

It was then that I realised that the poor dear was colour blind.

But he genuinely wants to please me, and so, when the roses arrived, he refused any responsibility as to their planting. Even when my husband and I had layered the trees of each variety in plots of earth apart from each other and explained into which bed we wanted each kind planted, he only wagged his old head doubtfully, chuckled, but did nothing.

Then Monsieur had an inspiration. He made a tour of the garden and collected bunches of fig-leaves, vine-leaves, lettuce-leaves, and others. Then he impaled a fig-leaf on the clump of ' Lamia ' roses and placed another fig-leaf upon the bed where the ' Lamia ' roses were to be planted, a vine-leaf on the ' Los Angeles ' clump and another on the bed designed for them, and so on. Then Hilaire, with a joyful shout of security and comprehension, set to work with feverish zeal.

" *Feuille de figue !* " he roared as he selected a ' Lamia ' rose and galloped to the corresponding leaf in the flower bed.

" *Feuille de vigne !* " he bellowed as he pulled out a ' Los Angeles,' and so on, till all our roses were planted in the right sequence of colour and in the right beds.

Our rose garden is now rather delicious, but, of

course, it owes much to its wonderful setting of
mountains and silvery olive groves. Oblong in
shape, it has two big square beds, each cut up in
the middle with stepping stones set amid grass. A
large round centre bed, with an old Provençal oil
jar planted with pink geraniums and blue plum-
bago in the middle of it, divides the two squares,
and round each bed is a border of grass flanked
by a little path of grey granite chips. Following
round the whole rose garden is a narrow rose
border edged with French lavender, and backed
on one side by the wall of the terrace above, and
on the other by vines overlooking the terrace
below. At the end of the rose garden I have
planted two cypresses (the tall pointed kind),
one for *La Paix* and one for *La Prospérité*, as is
the Provençal custom. (In passing I must mention
that *La Paix* was slightly nipped by the frost
soon after being planted, and when I remarked
on this to Hilaire, he informed me that the cypress
La Paix never prospered so well as its brother
because there *is* no peace in this world. Very
true, but it surprised me to learn that even trees
realised this painful truth.)

Under the two cypresses stands an ancient
table made of two huge chunks of stone—an ideal
place for tea, especially when our neighbour's
harvests of orange blossom or of jessamine are

Paix *and* Prospérité.

ready to be picked for the scent factories. One
day I mean to place a little statue of *Sainte Thérèse*
between the two cypresses, and train climbing
roses above and around her to represent the rain

of roses she prayed might fall upon mankind. But that must wait until the exchange improves— if ever it does!

I wanted so much to border my beds with little English pinks (why are they called *pinks* when they are really *whites?*), but Hilaire insisted upon grass, and grass in the South of France is nothing but a curse.

Monsieur and Madame, having left behind them acres upon acres of firm green turf, become impatient with Hilaire and his *gazon*. They never hear the end of it. First they must purchase expensive grass seed, and then for days Hilaire becomes engrossed in the preparation of the soil to receive it. After that the seed must be mixed with powdered manure, tenderly sprinkled upon the surface of the ground and watered daily. Hilaire becomes distracted when swarms of huge ants laboriously collect his grass seeds and pile them in heaps ready to be carried down to underground storehouses. With a wail of anguish he scatters the little mountains once more over the soil. This performance is repeated time and again while more important plants go hungry and thirsty. Pleas and protestations are of no avail. The *gazon* must first be served. " *L'un après l'autre,*" repeats Hilaire reprovingly.

It bores me to be obliged to carry with me a

plank of wood, lay it down, and walk on it whenever I want to pick flowers planted amid the
precious grass. It drives my husband to despair
when he is asked to buy expensive artificial encouragement for the *gazon*. With the depreciated
£, why waste money upon a few grass borders
which scorch up in August unless watered morning,
noon, and night, and must be dug up and planted
all over again in September? But grass apparently, good verdant grass, is a point of honour
among Provençal gardeners. They are snobbish
about their grass, and, whatever else suffers, the
gazon must be watered every day and cut at
least five times before anyone is allowed to walk
upon it.

We have got to have grass again this year.
We have replanned the garden in such a manner
that the minimum of grass seed will be required,
but we have not succeeded in avoiding it all.
The truth really is that I cannot bear to break
the heart of Hilaire. His life since the advent of
Monsieur and Madame last year, with their strange
English tastes, has been only too full of disappoint-
ments and discouragement in spite of their keen
desire to show him the affectionate appreciation
he so richly deserves. They do not mean to wound
him, but they can *not* stand his colour schemes or
his crowding. His idea of beauty is to plant

45

flowers of every hue in one shrieking discordant mass, and, when we first came, we used to wait till Sunday when his broad back was turned, and then, like two naughty children, dig up and transplant for all we were worth. On Monday mornings we braced ourselves and hardened our hearts to meet the reproachful eyes of Hilaire—dear, faithful, yellow-brown eyes like a spaniel's.

One day we bedded out some carnation cuttings —legitimate labour this time for which Hilaire had had no leisure. At last it was possible to see a few intervals of God's good red-brown earth between each plant instead of the close confusion of flowers elsewhere in the garden.

Next day, when we went out to gloat over our work, we found lines of mixed pansies, marigolds, and small button daisies completely covering the bed and jostling our poor carnations. Hilaire, beaming, told us that he had found the bed *triste*, and tried to enliven it.

But the vegetable and fruit garden is really Hilaire's kingdom where he reigns supreme, for we would not presume to make suggestions as to sowing in Provence. In England we did know something of the naughty little ways of vegetables, their likes and dislikes, their moods and caprices, but in Provence apparently they are more profligate, their appetites grosser, and their passions stronger.

I learned this first whilst watching Hilaire sowing peas and beans. He took each bean separately, wrapped it tenderly inside a ball of manure, and deposited it gently in a hole in the ground. Death to a fastidious English seed, but here in Provence they seem to like it ! When all the balls were buried, Hilaire watered the ground copiously, and then, wiping his horny hands on his blue apron, informed me that in a few days Madame would see green leaves pricking through the ground and in a few weeks beanstalks mounting to the clouds. It sounded to me rather like a fairy story I loved in my youth—but Hilaire was right.

He then proceeded to give me a lecture on the times and seasons for sowing. Everything, it seems, depends upon the moon. Beans and peas are amorous things, and must therefore be sown in the first quarter of the moon, for if they are sown while the lovely new moon is smiling down upon them, they spring towards her swiftly. During the last quarter, when her beauty is fading, they are less enthusiastic. Potatoes, carrots, and turnips, on the other hand, being, as I have always imagined, more phlegmatic in temperament, must be sown in the last quarter of the moon, who will drag their roots down for them as she sinks.

I shall never get used to the extraordinary growing powers of this climate and soil. I shall never cease to marvel when I find seeds planted on Monday pushing up leaves on Monday week. Hilaire set me to cut off *gourmandes* (suckers) from the tomatoes, and I filled two great baskets with them. I could hardly believe my eyes when a fortnight later he asked me to go over those tomatoes again, and I found as many *gourmandes* as before. In May, when I was walking with Monsieur Pierre in his olive groves picking masses of wild flowers as I went, we suddenly came into a clearing, and he pointed, silently, upwards. There stood two ancient olive-trees, at least 30 feet high, and rioting all over them, cascading and dripping from the gnarled branches at the very top, hung clusters of pale-yellow banksia roses, lovely and graceful against an azure sky. I gasped and stood amazed. Could they be roses climbing to that great height ? And then I remembered the remark of an English rose-grower : " Madam, you have never seen a climbing rose until you have seen it in the South of France. Here in England we haven't sun enough."

Monsieur Pierre regarded me with a look of amused contentment. He is proud of his banksia

roses ; he adores flowers and birds, and has
gained the reputation of a miser because, although
he has many *sous* in his stocking, he does not spend
them on gaieties of the town, but finds happiness
pottering among his flowers, his fruit-trees, his few
vegetables, his bees, and his birds. He showed
me a little rustic seat whereon he sits when eating
his simple *déjeuner*, and told me proudly that a
nightingale sang to him while he ate (they sing
day and night in Provence), and had actually
made her nest only three feet away.

Monsieur Pierre is a successful bee-keeper.
Honey is healthy stuff, fetches a good price in
the market, and, as he naïvely informs me, his
bees cost him nothing to feed, for are not the
terraces of jessamine and orange flowers belonging to our neighbour, Monsieur Jean, conveniently
near ? Talking of bees, he told me that a friend of
his imported queen bees from Germany, Egypt,
England, and America. The German bees, he
told me, always work overtime, and fill the cells
of the comb so full of honey that it reaches and
permeates the outer wax, thus spoiling the look
of the sections, so that they cannot be exhibited.
The Egyptian bees work well, but are fierce and
uncertain of temper—*méfiez-vous !* The English
bees work well, but only for a certain number of
hours ; and the American bees are brilliant but

" A nightingale sang to him while he ate his simple déjeuner."

erratic, sometimes working feverishly and sometimes taking a day off.

Extraordinary, I thought, that bees should have absorbed the characteristics of their countries.

I love Monsieur Pierre's philosophy of life. He stands before me clad in a grubby cotton shirt open at the throat, baggy cotton trousers secured over a vast and comfortable tumpkin by a worn leather belt, and a tiny black ' boater ' straw hat perched ridiculously above his kind moon face. He sweeps a brawny arm out towards the majesty of mountains rising above a sea of grey-green olive foliage, and asks me why people spend their lives striving to make money when *le bon Dieu* gives them all this beauty for nothing ? Is not health, and the life of a peasant in the open air, better than riches and a dyspeptic stomach in a city ? The world has grown too restless and discontented, and men have forgotten that peace and happiness can still be found in woods with birds and flowers and bees.

When I am with Monsieur Pierre I feel ashamed that the fallen £ has sometimes power to shake my poise. I have a deep respect for Monsieur Pierre.

Hilaire, on the contrary, despises him heartily. Monsieur Pierre lets all his *planches* (terraces) run wild. His ground is nothing but a wilderness, whereas good vegetables could be grown—and sold well—by an industrious man where now there is only a carpet of wild flowers. Hilaire snorts when Monsieur Pierre rolls up our drive in the cool of the evening clasping a bouquet of these despised *fleurs sauvages* against his ponderous middle—a gift for Madame. Madame has a garden of her own, has she not ? And does not Hilaire grow fine marigolds, antirrhinums, stocks, and geraniums for her delight ? Indeed he does ! But those humble posies of Monsieur Pierre's are precious to her nevertheless.

Oh, the wild flowers of Provence ! ` My first spring here was like a dream come true. In the autumn we had laboriously planted thousands of bulbs imported, expensively, from Holland. These we planted under the scornful eye of Hilaire, who refused to be interested in them—we wondered why. When spring burst upon us one perfect morning (nothing comes gradually in Provence), I found the grassy terraces under the olive-trees one sheet of tiny blue Roman hyacinths, miniature scarlet tulips, mauve and scarlet anemones, and yellow jonquils. When I exclaimed in delight to Hilaire that our predecessor here had planted lavishly and beautifully, he at first looked blank, and then, when I pointed rapturously to the jewelled grass on the terraces below, he gave it one contemptuous glance and said, " *Ah ça !— sont sauvages, Madame.*"

Wild tulips, hyacinths, anemones, and jonquils !

Smaller, of course, than the tame ones from Holland, but, to my mind, infinitely more fragrant, delicate, and lovely. Little wonder that Hilaire had watched our bulb-planting with pitying eyes !

And so it went on all the year through, one luxuriant sequence of wild flowers, carefully culti-vated in English gardens, but here claiming gloriously every mountain and valley for their own. The meek inheriting the earth. In May, the white Mediterranean heath, growing to a height of six feet in certain corners of the Esterels, covering the mountains like drifts of snow ; patches of hepaticas, tiny yellow tulips, bee orchis, and every kind of orchis. In June, the scented acres of Spanish broom, its strong green spikes sprinkled with blossoms like great golden butterflies (and how I cherished proudly one bush of Spanish broom in my Hertfordshire garden, and almost wept when untimely pruning killed it). In July, the mountains covered with misty mauve lavender ; pink and white creeping phlox ; rose-mary ; tussocks of thyme, white, pink, and purple ; great bushes of *cyste* and clumps of the loveliest blue star-flower whose name I do not know. And in August, blossoming myrtle, honeysuckle, sweet peas, dianthus, and clematis. A friend of mine collected sixty-three varieties of wild flowers in one short hour on the mountains and came to me for a botany book to identify them—a task impossible in an English book, for there are greater treasures found in the hot sunshine and mountains of Provence.

And we strive to make gardens in the South of France! Why bother, when Nature makes the whole country into one glorious garden and plants for us on so lavish and varied a scale?

But then if I had no garden I should have no Hilaire, and without him life would be far less happy and amusing. From the first moment, when the vendor of this property introduced him to me, I loved Hilaire and he loved me. Would we take over Hilaire with the property? "*C'est un brave homme—travailleur—très devoué*," and then from a terrace above us I became conscious of two anxious golden-brown eyes looking down into mine with an expression of dumb pleading. Instinctively my face softened into a reassuring smile. Then I saw those spaniel eyes light up, and as though I had called him with my glance, Hilaire climbed slowly down the stairway towards me, never taking his eyes from my face. I held out my hand to him, asking him if he would stay on and take care of the garden, Monsieur, and me.

He had bared his old head as he approached, and now he took my hand in both his hard brown paws and bent his head low over it as he thanked me, rather as though swearing fealty to a queen. Then he straightened himself and gave me a long look of promise and fidelity in the eyes. He did the same to Monsieur, and so the bargain was sealed.

Hilaire is fifty-six, but he looks very much older, for did he not live through the Dardanelles campaign ? Was he not squatting in a trench when he saw the beloved General Gouraud blown many metres into the air by the shell which maimed him ? And all the time, like thousands of other French *poilus*, Hilaire was homesick for his young wife and little son of five years old ; so longing for them and so anxious for their fate should he be sent to *le bon Dieu* prematurely by just such another shell as that which wounded his gallant General, that his luxuriant crop of hair began to fall. I have since seen a terrible wooden-faced portrait of Hilaire with a curly ' quiff ' on his brow, taken by the side of an equally wooden-faced wife, which hangs triumphantly conspicuous in the centre of their parlour wall. This proves conclusively that his dear bald head used to be covered once upon a time. He regrets those fallen locks, and will not believe me when I assure him that he is much better-looking now than then. A fine high brow has Hilaire above those faithful golden eyes with their wistful expression, and below them a good nose and chin. In a hat he looks quite young ; without one, when he turns his back and displays the white circle of baldness on the crown where the sun has not burnt him brown, he might be sixty-six or more.

After the Dardanelles, Salonica—and dysentery. Then an English hospital at Cannes, where Hilaire spent the happiest months of his life. Oh ! the way those English nurses washed one. They were always at it. Clean sheets and clean nightshirt every day. " *Ah ! la-la !* " and Hilaire wrings his hands and laughs all over his face. And the food ! *How* he was fed ! His face became round as the moon at full, and each week he put on another *kilo* of weight. And every day kind English ladies brought the French soldiers cigarettes, flowers, newspapers, and books, or came and took them for drives and picnics when they were convalescent. Ah ! all the French soldiers were *bien gâtés*—and they enjoyed being spoiled enormously, as we all do. Then, Madame Hilaire and *le petit* came down from the mountains once a week to say " *Bon jour.*" One was sorry to leave that hospital —" *On était bien là !* "

From these confidences it will be gathered that Hilaire, Monsieur, and Madame had become fast friends. I have since been informed that had Hilaire not liked us our life here would have been hell. All our peasant neighbours are his relations, and, had he not considered us *gentille*, our fruit, flowers, and vegetables, even our hens, pigeons, and rabbits, would never have been safe. As it is, not a flower has ever been touched, and I am the constant recipient of little gifts from my neighbours : a pair of pigeons, a spray of orange-blossom, a basket of cherries, or *oranges sauvages*. And our garden is constantly being embellished by plants from some mysterious source. Suddenly I find a bed of purple stocks—and I did not buy them. Hilaire is asked from whence they come, and replies with a shrug and a grin, " *Un ami, Madame.*" A friendly country, this Provence. On certain cottage doors are hung little baskets, or a wooden *sabot*, and into these it is customary sometimes to place a small gift in passing—an egg, a bunch of flowers, an orange, or any little anonymous token of friendship. I suppose because I have not had the effrontery to hang a basket on my door, these little gifts of plants and seed are given to Hilaire to plant surreptitiously to give me the joy of surprise.

How these Provençal gardeners work ! Hilaire, during the heat of August, was here at 5.30 A.M. watering the garden. With difficulty did we at last persuade him to take two hours' rest in the middle of the day, and at 2 P.M. there he was, back again, hard at work in the sweltering heat, and here he remained till darkness fell. They work also on Sunday mornings. When I protested, Hilaire implored me to let him come. *Le bon Dieu*, Hilaire was sure, did not love to see the fruits of His earth die for want of care. And what was

"*A letter . . . marked 'Urgent.'*"

there for a gardener to do at home, shut indoors on a lovely morning? Hilaire was no scholar, he informed me, and to read the newspaper was pain. He preferred to work in the garden till eleven o'clock, and then he would go home *faire la toilette*. He becomes ten years younger when that unsightly week's growth of beard is removed, and I like him best on Mondays.

No! Hilaire is not a scholar. After our flying visit in June last year to buy the little property, a letter sent on from England for me and marked 'Urgent' was brought to Hilaire. The postman told him that it was an important letter, and so Hilaire tied it up in his cotton handkerchief where all his money and valuables are secured, and kept it ever about his person so that it might be safe for Madame on her return in September.

When she came, with great pride he produced it, reduced to a smeared and pulpy condition from constant contact with hot skin, but safe for all that. In four months it had, of course, answered itself.

But though Hilaire is no student of books, he is very, very wise, and wisdom I have learned to consider of more value than knowledge. He has an instinct for weather which is almost animal and quite unerring, helped by natural signs and portents. A snail has walked across a path with only one horn extended—Hilaire abandons his watering of the garden, for it will certainly rain. It does. Carrion crows come flying down from the heights into the valleys—there will be a storm, for the crows know this beforehand and leave the wild parts of the mountains to seek shelter in the woods below. There is a storm. The *cigale* has been heard in the olive groves—*la grande chaleur commence*, and sure enough summer has come next day and the great heat.

To see Hilaire among the birds and beasts of our little domaine is to see him at his best.

" Tee-tee-tee-teeeeeeeeeeeee ! " he calls to them softly, and baby rabbits appear, expectant, with pricked ears. As they gambol round him Hilaire laughs and laughs with pleasure. The rabbits are kept for utility purposes—*lapin au vin blanc* is excellent, and the hotel near-by likes to buy home-fed rabbits. For this reason Madame avoids those alluring baby rabbits, knowing that later she must harden her heart and pronounce the death sentence. But then it will be Emilia, the practical, who will massacre the innocents, for Hilaire, with his golden eyes swimming and a tragic gesture of the hands, pleads with Madame, " *Moi, je ne peux pas—c'est moi qui les soigne, Madame.*" Caring for them daily he has grown to love them, and he cannot betray them now. And Madame well understands.

The queer *pigeons du pays* with their feathered legs all know him, and I am called to see a new pair of babies in the nest. Is there anything more hideous than a baby pigeon, all eyes and beak and a most disgusting baldness ? But Hilaire thinks them beautiful. He tells me that the papa pigeon is now making love to another woman, and I express intense indignation. I prefer faithful husbands and strongly object to such goings-on in my pigeon-cote. Hilaire laughs until he chokes : " *C'est la vie, Madame,*" he gasps, " *et elle est belle, vous savez !* " jerking a knowing thumb at the shameless flirt who is alienating the affections of the husband while his true wife is in child-bed.

The chickens are fed ; hot eggs are removed

from under a furious broody hen who, though twice soused in the fountain by Hilaire to cool her ardour, persists still in sitting on the egg-box. The rabbits are collected from various holes in the wall and shooed from their yard into an inner sanctuary safe from predatory and starving cats, and Hilaire, locking all doors, hides the keys in some new place. Sometimes it is in a flower-pot, sometimes under a boulder or a pile of sand, but never in the same place, as Monsieur and Madame have learned to their exasperation on Sunday evenings when Hilaire is away.

Then he climbs from terrace to terrace, giving a twist to each water-tap lest any precious water should trickle away in the night ; casts a loving eye over the little domaine drowsing in the after-glow, and one last glance at his latest piece of work—a rustic Provençal stairway of stone slabs. He sees that it is good, slings his food-bag over his shoulder, and clumps down the terraces to the little garden gate leading to his home amid the olive groves.

As he trudges along he passes Monsieur and Madame, who are dining on the terrace of the rose garden near the little cascade. They raise their glasses to him.

" *Bon soir, Hilaire, bonne nuit !* "

" Bon soir, Monsieur-et-dame. Bon appétit ! "

For a moment they see his wrinkled brown face and golden eyes smiling at them through the pergola, and then the circle of baldness on his dear old crown as he turns away and lumbers wearily off into the dim silence of the olive groves.

MARRIAGE.

I WAS caught—under my own mosquito-net! I had decided to be a real lady for once, go to bed early, and have my dinner brought to me, being thoroughly tired out by the unprecedented heat wave in Provence.

Having demolished my dinner, I lay luxuriously staring out of my windows at a mass of mountains gradually fading away into an opalescent dusk, when there came a knock at my door and Emilia entered.

Her merry little face wore a curious mixture of expressions. I have learned to know that face very well, and I thought that I read in it now the importance of withheld information that she could impart if she would, a certain hostility towards someone (not me) and a kind of mock humility of manner as she announced that Madame Hippolyte begged the honour of a private word with Madame.

Now Madame Hippolyte is one of our peasant neighbours. Her husband sells wood and manure —both scarce and costly in Provence—so that he makes a very good thing out of it, and Madame Hippolyte is rather apt to wear a proud look and a high tumpkin in consequence. Hence Emilia's mixture of expressions when she announced the ambitious lady.

" But what an hour to come, Emilia ! " I objected. " Did you say that Madame was in bed ? "

Oh yes, Madame Hippolyte had been informed that Madame was in bed ; but it appeared that her business was of the most pressing and private nature. Emilia tossed her buzzle head and folded her little fat hands before her.

" Oh well, show her up to my room," I replied wearily, " but explain that Madame is *fatiguée* and cannot see her for long."

I knew that this warning would be perfectly impotent to stop the flood of Madame Hippolyte's eloquence once it began to flow, and I lay back on my pillows in resigned expectation.

In she came, a black cashmere shawl thrown negligently over her shoulders, her grey hair neatly brushed, wearing shoes instead of *pantoufles* (the news she had to impart must therefore be important), and a look of excitement and cunning in her black beady eyes.

Of course, she was desolated to find Madame in bed—she hoped from her heart that it was nothing serious ? Only a matter of the utmost importance would have emboldened her to disturb Madame at such an hour. But *la petite*, it appeared, was to be married—but yes! quite soon. Her papa had at last given his consent. True, the young couple were too young, and it was sad to lose a daughter of hardly seventeen, but—what would you? An expressive gesture of two brown arms.

Madame Hippolyte explained that she had come herself to invite Madame to the *mariage*, and, if Madame would so honour the family, to *le repas* afterwards. Madame Hippolyte would strive her hardest to find *un beau cavalier* to walk with Madame in the wedding procession—that is to say, if Monsieur could not be prevailed upon to accompany Madame?

This last suggestion was made in a very sly and hopeful manner. It would be a great *coup* to secure Monsieur too, known to be a recluse and a *savant*. The Hippolyte stock would rise even higher in the market.

I thanked Madame Hippolyte very heartily for the compliment she and her family paid to me, and said that it would give me the greatest pleasure to go to the church, informally, to see the little Mademoiselle Marguerite married to her gallant *Chasseur Alpin*, but that not being a relation, I could on no account join in the wedding pro-

" It was sad to lose a daughter of hardly seventeen."

cession. Monsieur I excused altogether on the
score of much literary work.

But surely Madame would come to the wedding breakfast afterwards, pleaded Madame Hippolyte. It would be done in the best manner; the villa of a kind neighbouring lady who was away for the summer had been lent for the occasion, and her cook would furnish the meal—a great saving for poor people like themselves, for *" Ah la la ! "* what an expensive thing a marriage was ! There were the cars to hire, and at least two would be necessary. They thought of hiring the smart Fiat of Monsieur Georges in the town. That would hold the *filles d'honneur*, but the problem was to find another Fiat car, equally *chic*, to take the *jeunes mariés*, for it would be such a pity if all were not *en suite*.

PAUSE...................

Madame Hippolyte, her head on one side, looked at me fixedly with her cunning little eyes under narrowed lids. Only her fingers, pleating her black dress, betrayed her suppressed excitement.

At the word ' Fiat ' the hidden meaning of this mysterious late visit dawned upon me, also of Emilia's demeanour when she announced the visitor.

MINE was a Fiat car—a very smart new saloon in a shade of *grenat*. It would comfortably accommodate, first, the bride and her father, and later

the married couple. I was being slowly mes-
merised to offer it, and, having offered it, to drive
it myself, for we have no *chauffeur*. The Hippolyte
family would thus secure not only a car free of
charge, but also the presence of Madame who must
drive it.

I decided that this might be rather an amusing
adventure, and I liked the young couple ; therefore, very innocently, as though quite unaware
of the trap laid for me, I walked into it voluntarily.

" I will lend you my car if you like, Madame
Hippolyte," I said heartily. " I shall be delighted
to drive your pretty daughter to the church."

The black eyes of Madame Hippolyte snapped
with triumph. I had swallowed the bait ; she
had caught her fish—under a mosquito-net. Of
course, she was overwhelmed with surprise and
joy. Was Madame's car indeed a Fiat ? She
had forgotten that Madame had a car ! How
very wonderful and extraordinary ! *Quel coin-
cidence !* How could she ever thank Madame
enough ? But it was well known that Madame
had *un bon cœur*. Hippolyte would be overwhelmed—Marguerite enchanted ! It was a piece
of such unlooked-for good fortune for them, and
what an economy when *sous* were so scarce.

Her object attained she rose briskly to her feet :
she could not think of tiring Madame any longer,

but Madame had always been so kind that she must be one of the very first to know of Marguerite's imminent marriage. If Monsieur and Madame could not come to *le repas*, at least they would not withhold the light of their countenances at *le dessert?* The young people would make merry and dance after the wedding breakfast — and so on.

Madame smiled but did not commit herself. She felt that having acted as *chauffeuse* to and from the church her duty would be well and truly done, and that nothing more could, in equity, be demanded of her.

Having voiced her last plea, Madame Hippolyte bustled off. Emilia, coming in afterwards for my dinner-tray, had a tight mouth, a flushed face, and an extremely indignant look in her eyes. Being a peasant herself, she knew exactly why Madame Hippolyte had descended upon me. Emilia very evidently thought both the visit and its object ' cheek '—or its Italian equivalent— and was bursting to have an opportunity to say so. She did not get it. Italians have not yet learned to love the French, and Italians hate all vainglory and pretension. They also—if they love their employers—hate them to be ' put upon,' and Madame had no intention of explaining that her capitulation was voluntary, and that, like

Emilia, she had seen through Madame Hippolyte's device.

During the days which intervened before the marriage we had several visits from various members of, and prospective relations to, the Hippolyte family. The son of the house, whilst depositing a load of logs in our shed, asked for Madame to sign a delivery note, and casually remarked that a neighbour was going to supply white flowers for the banqueting table on the wedding day, but feared that she would not have enough to decorate the bridal car (MINE).

PAUSE....................

" Ha, ha ! " thought I, " then I am supposed to supply white flowers and to garland my car. I hadn't realised that."

Aloud I said what was expected of me. " Of course, I shall supply white flowers to decorate my own car. How is it done ? I want to do the right thing in the right way."

The youth's ingenuous face brightened. If Madame would just order a few dozen white carnations (out of season and extremely costly) at Garondi's (the most expensive florist in the town), and just a pretty bouquet of lilies and roses arranged in a small basket to be hung between the two front seats, and a few garlands of smilax and asparagus fern, the Hippolyte family would do all the decorating. They could not think of giving Madame the trouble of doing it herself or the expense of getting Monsieur Garondi to do it. Of course, Madame, who had been already so kind and generous, could not be expected to do decorations for the family wedding. Indeed, if Madame liked, he would go himself to Garondi's on his way home and give the order for the few flowers himself and so save Madame the trouble of going *en ville*.

In parting, he announced to me the intention of the young engaged couple of paying us their respects and expressing their gratitude in the matter of the car before the wedding. His mother hoped much, he said, that we would walk up through the olive groves to their humble abode and see *le grand tas* of wedding presents that Marguerite had already received, but Marguerite would repeat the invitation herself when she brought her *fiancé* to be presented to Monsieur and Madame. Perhaps to-morrow evening might be convenient to Monsieur and Madame ?

The young couple duly arrived after dinner next day, just in time for coffee and a *cognac* (our gardener lodges on the top floor of the Hippolyte mansion and knows well our habits and our hours), and, of course, received from us the expected wedding present. Marguerite was terribly smart, with a brilliantly tinted face like a *Parisienne* and a ridiculous little *à la mode* hat perched on her raven hair and tilted well over the right eye. Her *Chasseur Alpin* was quite a good specimen, sturdily built, with a good clear eye and a manner both respectful and easy. Quite obviously he adored his Marguerite, and she, little *coquette*, pretended to ignore the fact that he never took his eyes off her pretty painted face. She affected manners to match her complexion, cast sidelong glances at *Monsieur* under her long lashes, made little *moues* with her brightly salved lips and was very cool and off-hand with her lover — little minx !

When I presented our small gift—a bit of silver-plate—she condescended to say " *Ce n'est pas mal*," while her *fiancé* fingered it reverently and thanked us for our thought of them.

Next day the future mother-in-law and sister-in-law appeared to pay their homage to Madame, and incidentally to see over her new house and garden, the fame of which, spread by the boastful Emilia, had reached their distant village. They thought it only right that the future relations of our neighbours should early make themselves known to us. Marguerite's future mother-in-law informed me acidly that the bridal dress (white

satin) had been tried on that day ; that her son
had refused to stand in church beside a bride in
so *décolleté* a gown ; that a *modestie* must be inserted, or that the marriage could not go forward.
There had been a scene. Marguerite was in tears
(of rage). She had a temper, that girl, and *le bon*

" *Hippolyte père in a rickety cart drawn by a vicious mule.*"

Dieu only knew if she were capable of making a
good son a worthy wife. *Hélas !* and so on. I
thought they would never go.

A few days later came Hippolyte *père* in a rickety
cart drawn by a vicious mule. He came ostensibly
to thank us for the promised loan of the car and
to try to persuade Monsieur to leave his books
on the great marriage day and honour the house

of Hippolyte with his presence. In parting he happened to remark that the whole neighbourhood seemed to be laying in a stock of logs for the winter—at summer prices—and he was kept so busy delivering wood that he hardly had time to attend to the business of the wedding. But it was prudent of these people to order logs now, because wood was very scarce, and customers who were late with their commands would not get served at all. The supply was already very low.

Monsieur, in apprehension, hastily ordered several hundreds of logs, and Hippolyte drove off happily, and doubtless told his ugly mule on the homeward way that the order of Monsieur would cover the hire of that extra Fiat car and all the wedding breakfast.

The day before the wedding, Hippolyte's woodcutter lumbered down to ask Madame if she would kindly see that her car was outside the Hippolyte abode by 9 A.M. next day, so that it might be decorated in good time for the ceremony at the church at 10.30.

I did some quick thinking. If I drove the car up to the Hippolyte house along the main road at that early hour, and left it there during the process of decoration, I must return on foot by a short-cut (through damp olive groves and over a stony mountain track) if I were to allow enough time to change into the wedding finery that was obviously expected of me. Then I must walk back again in my flimsy attire (a good kilometre and a half) in time to take my seat at the wheel and drive to the church. There seemed nothing for it but to dress myself early, drive up the car and wait in the Hippolyte mansion till my services were required. A full hour to be spent in the company of the bride's and bridegroom's relations and friends in a stuffy cottage, making polite conversation in halting French, Provençal, and Italian! What a prospect! WHY had I done this thing? What a boomerang it was proving! And they were certain to have flavoured their *petit déjeuner* with garlic.

However, I had not yet inspected *le tas* of wedding presents, and that would occupy some of the time. I devoutly hoped that my stock of French adjectives would not give out too soon.

On the eventful morning I arrayed myself in a white *crêpe-de-Chine* frock sprigged all over with pale blue flowers and a big floppy white hat (so depressing in the early morning!) and drove up to *Maison Hippolyte*.

Outside the cottage was already assembled a small crowd looking (and perhaps feeling) as miserable as I felt in their ' best clothes ' at that hour in the morning. They all stood about silent and depressed, as though attired for *pompe funèbre* and awaiting the arrival of a funeral coach instead of my bridal car.

Monsieur Hippolyte lurched forward to meet me. He was not yet fully dressed, having wisely decided not to put on his collar, tie, waistcoat, or boots till the last moment. So would he be freer to imbibe *apéritifs*, smoke cheap cigars, and entertain his relatives and guests, packed into a room six feet by four with the only window closed.

He greeted me very charmingly, helped me to alight, and immediately my car was seized upon by amateur florists bristling with pins, which were stuck all down the lapels of their coats. My poor upholstery !

I was led into that airless room, and was nearly knocked down upon entry by the combined fumes of *caporal* cigarettes, Italian cheroots, cheap perfumery (there were ladies present), garlic, *cognac*, bananas (there were several children in the room), boot-blacking, hair-oil, hot clothes—and people.

I was then introduced to all the bride's relations and also those of the bridegroom, to the *filles d'honneur* and their *cavaliers*.

" *Comment ça va ?   Ça va bien ?* " a score of times accompanied by sticky handshakings, for the day was hot. I then was placed in a hard kitchen chair in the middle of the tiny room, like a prize pig in a pen, surrounded by appraising eyes, exactly in front of a small deal table covered with *casseroles*, cups and saucers, articles of *lingerie*, &c.—*le tas* of wedding presents. Foremost was placed our tiny piece of silver-plate. It looked to me very insignificant against a background of shining saucepans, but I had Mademoiselle Marguerite's kind assurance " *Ce n'est pas mal* " to comfort me.

I complimented Madame Hippolyte, still *en peignoir* and curlers, upon these practical gifts, and then turned to the grandfather of the bridegroom, who was almost plastered on my back, so close was the crowd. He had come from Marseille the night before, he informed me, travelling all night in spite of his seventy-six years. There he sat, blinking a little sleepily but stiffly erect in his awful black clothes, with a gigantic white buttonhole like a small cauliflower. His hair was shaved for the summer, but the knobs of his head shone wet in spite of this. He pointed out the fruit of his loins, clustered like tomatoes around him with faces inflamed with heat. There was Pierre, the eldest, conspicuous by two merry brown eyes, a round head going rapidly bald, a smart pointed moustache, and a comfortable tumpkin adorned by a metal cable to which, I supposed, a massive watch was attached. The lapel of his coat showed a wonderful array of war ribbons, and, in spite of his growing girth, he bore himself like a soldier worthy of a *Chasseur Alpin* son, already a *Sergent-Chef*, for he was the father of the bridegroom.

Five other sons there were, and goodness knows how many grandsons and granddaughters crawling under tables and chairs and racing up and down the staircase. Just to make conversation, I informed *Grand-Père* that Monsieur (my Monsieur) was the fifth son of his family, and that his father had had fourteen children.

" *Un bon coq!* " ejaculated *Grand-Père* admiringly, which completely dried up my eloquence.

The awkward silence was broken by the entrance of one of the *filles d'honneur*, who coquettishly offered buttonholes (some of my white carnations filched from the car) to the *cavaliers*, all *Chasseurs Alpins*. The usual exchange of gallantries and blushes ; the usual demand that the *demoiselle charmante* should fix the flower in place ; the usual frantic search for pins, which were not forthcoming until an obliging matron pulled up her skirt and extracted several which were keeping up the hem of her torn and rather dirty petticoat under a very smart dress, and at last all the soldiers were decorated. One of them admired the red rose worn in the ample bosom of the mother of the

78

bridegroom. He said it was such a beautiful shade of *yellow*—and laughed. When she protested that the colour was *rouge vif*, he informed us that the *Chasseurs Alpins* were never allowed to name that colour save in three connections—blood, the red of the French flag, and a woman's lips. Curious.

Whilst we were all trussed cosily together in that little oven, slowly cooking and simmering until the hour of ten should strike, I occasionally caught glimpses of the bride on the staircase *en déshabille*, flirting with her boy friends and relations. There were sudden assaults, stolen kisses, muffled shrieks, and slaps as Mademoiselle Marguerite coquetted for the last time as a spinster. I felt sure that it would not be the last time in her life. Her future husband was safely superintending the adornment of the bridal car outside the cottage, so the field was free.

But when she finally appeared, robed in the white satin gown—WITH *modestie* affixed—she descended the staircase with the timid shy air of a virgin about to take the most important step of her life. It was very artistically done. She had refrained from painting her pretty face, which was only lavishly powdered and the lips slightly reddened to accentuate the appropriate pallor expected at weddings, and she stood in the hall, apparently unaware of the goggling eyes of ad-

79

miration fixed upon her by the assembled crowd,
looking nervously around for her father.

Monsieur Hippolyte, who had been drinking
apéritif after *apéritif*, joking and laughing and
digging the ribs of the comrades of his youth and
generally having a high old time, suddenly appeared
coated, waistcoated, collared, and booted, with
a heavy sad step and a furrowed brow, and the
expression of a father about to be bereaved of
his only daughter.

With a fixed tragic look at her, he offered her
his arm with a semi-reluctant trembling gesture,
and together they passed silently and slowly
out of the house. It was admirably done. Mr
Vincent Crummles and Miss Henrietta Petowker
themselves, though both of them in ' the profession,' could not have played their parts better.
The French have a great sense of drama.

The *chauffeuse* saw that her moment had come,
sprang to her feet, walked diffidently behind the
important pair, and took her place at the wheel.
My car had been decorated, regardless of (my)
expense, with the flowers so kindly ordered from
Garondi's on my behalf by Hippolyte *fils*, and
we entered a very bower of white carnations and
smilax. Every time I turned the wheel my elbow
bumped against the ' outsize ' floral basket hung
between the front *fauteuils*.

The drive was accomplished in complete silence. I have driven for years, but never before have I been so nervous. I realised that if I skidded over the edge of a ravine—there would be no wedding. *On me* depended the success of the occasion. Nevertheless, when we were on the flat, I could still enjoy the glimpses I got of Monsieur Hippo-

" My car had been decorated."

lyte's gloomy face as he stared before him, and Mademoiselle Marguerite's downcast eyes reflected in the mirror before mine. The pair appeared quite unconscious of the inquisitive faces that lined the route. As a spectacle a wedding is second-best only to a funeral all the world over.

We bumped down the final twisty mountain road, descended upon La Place, and I threaded my way through a crowd of peasants to the doors of the Mairie, opposite the church. There we waited until the *filles d'honneur* and their *cavaliers* drew up in the other Fiat ; a Noah's ark procession was formed and they all entered in, the faltering bride upon her father's trembling arm.

Then I, as *chauffeuse*, swung the car round into the shade of the bobbed-headed plane-trees, parked her, and got out, assisted to alight by the *Capitaine* of the *Chasseurs Alpins* and his smart *Lieutenant* who had come to see their *Sergent-Chef* happily married, and who confided to me that " *La petite avait de la chance* " because the bridegroom was a splendid fellow.

The mysteries in the Mairie having been performed, the procession came out and went into the church, where the Marriage Mass was celebrated by a dear old toothless priest before a congregation far more reverent than is ever seen nowadays at English weddings, where the church generally becomes a theatre, with intervals for music and conversation during the performance. During a pause in this service one of the *filles d'honneur* visited us all with a tiny embroidered bag made from a strip of the same material as the bride's gown, to collect *sous* for some charity.

Being a *mariage à la mode* and done in the best style, of course there was the usual Press photographer waiting outside the church to take pictures of the wedding. Unfortunately, just as the bride was conscious of the apparatus focussed upon her and was casting a tender glance at her groom, she tripped on a stone and stumbled, thereby spoiling the only plate of the local photographer, who was perhaps even more furious than she was.

I was by this time rather tired and hot—and very hungry—but I was upheld by the thought that my duty was nearly done as I drove the *nouveaux mariés* towards the ancestral mansion, when, to my utmost consternation, the bridegroom leaned forward and asked very charmingly if Madame would be so very kind as to drive them to the town to have their photographs properly taken with their attendants.

It had evidently been a prearranged thing, for the Fiat containing the *filles d'honneur* and *cavaliers* shot past us and the Hippolyte cottage on its way to the town while I was slowing up to hear what the *Sergent-Chef* had to say.

How could I refuse? As I drove onward those three kilometres to the town, I had regretful visions of an overdone chicken and an irate husband to greet me on my belated return.

The photography did not take quite so long as I had feared, and I was only one and a half hours late for luncheon when at length I reached home.

after waiting for the car to be dismantled from its decorations, which were afterwards used to adorn the marriage feast and for a battle of flowers.

The family had made such a point of the presence of both Monsieur and Madame at *le dessert* that we felt that we must at least put in an appearance, even if we only stayed five minutes. But we waited till half-past three, thinking that by that time the feasting would be over and we should see the young people dancing—in another room and atmosphere.

But, oh no! When we arrived they were still hard at it, and, as we entered the hall of the lent house, we heard the strains of a high falsetto voice singing some doleful ballad excruciatingly out of tune.

Monsieur Hippolyte spied us from afar and shuffled forward to meet us in his new and painfully tight boots, twisting his agonised face into an expression of delight. The whole company broke off at our entrance and gave us the usual welcome of clapping. Five strokes of the right palm on the left, five strokes of the left palm on the right, five more on the right with the left and then three short sharp claps before the face.

We were then placed in seats of honour, and the bride cut us a piece of her extremely sticky wedding-cake—a kind of crisp batter dipped in toffee and filled with whipped cream. On its summit stood two little dolls dressed as bride and bridegroom.

Monsieur, greatly daring, was in the act of conveying a glutinous spoonful to his mouth when hit in the eye by the head of a white carnation, which displaced his eyeglass into his plate. His look of indignant surprise changed into a broad smile when he discovered that the compliment came from one of the pretty bridesmaids, and was merely the opening shot of an ensuing battle of flowers. Champagne corks popped, flowers flew through the heated air, *cavaliers* chanted dirges saluted by volleys of the Provençal clapping, and all present became even more flushed and sticky and gay.

Monsieur was marvellous. He could not face the champagne, but he did swallow the cake. He flirted with puce-faced matrons, he shied carnations at pretty girls. I believe he would even have sung—if asked. He was the great surprise and success of *le dessert*, he who was known to be such a recluse and *savant !*

I think his great regret was that he could not join in the dancing. Two wheezy gramophones replaced each other as orchestra, and the bride and bridegroom opened the ball by dancing a tango quite deliciously. Both were real artists.

and it was a joy to watch them. I was delighted
when later the *Sergent-Chef* asked me to dance

" Champagne corks popped."

with him while his bride sinuously revolved with
the best man. I had hoped for a waltz—to my
mind the only dance worth dancing—but when I

saw the Provençal variety I funked it. The great
art is, it seems, to see how many swift revolutions
a couple can make in the shortest time *upon one
spot*. Just a tee-to-tum whirling continuously.
It made me giddy even to watch the couple who
had gained the first prize in a *Concours de Danse*
that season. I forget how many revolutions they
had made to the minute to gain that distinction.

Less practised and professional were the antics
of the bridegroom's father, who danced round the
room with a mop, saying that it was more tractable
and quiet than any woman, and using it at intervals
to sweep away confetti, carnation heads, and paper
ribbons from the dancing-floor.

Grand-Père fell stertorously asleep. The long
journey, followed by such excitement and much
wine, proved at last too much for his waking
powers. We were exhausted after only two hours
of these festivities in that atmosphere, but we
heard afterwards that the bridal party 'kept it
up' till 1.30 A.M., when the happy pair drove off
(thank God, *in the other* Fiat car) to their new
appartement in the town.

The feasting and rejoicings were continued for
the whole of the next day, it being a Sunday
and a holiday for everybody. Besides, the thrifty
French wanted to make quite sure that no crumb
of the provisions and no drop of the wedding

wine were wasted. We were invited once more, but simply could not face the anticlimax and forced gaiety of that aftermath, and so excused ourselves and stayed quietly at home.

Hippolyte *père* has been in bed ever since with a fierce and prolonged attack of gout—small wonder !

Madame Hippolyte came to visit us early after the celebrations to thank us for all our kindness, bringing with her her plebeian lady rabbit to be married (without previously having asked or gained our consent to the union) to our pedigree buck.

BUSINESS.

IF business is business in other parts of the world, here in Provence it is fun.

Let those who complain of the snatch-and-grab methods of commerce in this century, and the rush and hustle of modern life, come and shop with me in a Provençal town.

Here there is a lovely leisure in all our doings. The sun shines so gloriously, the sky is so incredibly blue, and the scent of flowers, warmed by the sunshine, so drowsy and intoxicating that there is every inducement to be lazy and leisurely.

A stranger without humour might perhaps be maddened by the ways of the Provençaux, but he whom God has endowed with much patience and a little humour will enjoy them.

For a shopping expedition here, one also requires a large and capacious string bag. Foreigners coming to Provence are apt to line their string bags with some attractive colour, thus protecting their purchases from dust and rain and modestly concealing their household supplies. Not so the Provençaux, who prefer an unveiled bag so as to allow the fat carrots, stout leeks, rotund cabbages, and other prizes filched from under the very noses of early-rising and enterprising *bonnes* in the market to raise the envy of the defeated.

To return home, staggering under the weight

Shopping in Provence.

of a string bag bursting with purchases, is far more satisfactory than the surreptitious shopping of the uninitiated. There is a touch of distinction in the scaly leg of a fine chicken sticking out triumphantly through the meshes, or (if the *bonne* be shopping for a French household) a live rabbit squealing and squiggling within it, poor beastie, as proof to Madame, when it makes its eventual appearance stewed in white or red wine, that it is really fresh meat. If both hands are occupied, the right holding the string bag and the left grasping an equally bulky one of American cloth, one is proud indeed, for one represents a well-furnished house with a well-replenished larder. That is the viewpoint of the *bonne*. There is snobbery even in shopping.

To appear in the market without a *filet* (string bag) is deeply resented by the vendors. That I learned early. Packing-paper is rare and local newspapers are sparsely paged; string is almost unknown, and raffia costs money. I was regarded with a reproachful eye; I was marked down as a novice; and, as I was informed by Emilia on my return, the price of the vendor's time wasted in packing up my purchases was added to the bill for goods supplied. It is cheaper far to carry a string bag when shopping in Provence.

I was also taught that when marketing one should never be content with the goods displayed on the stalls. The more difficult Madame is, the more she will be respected. Very soon I learned to bend the beaks and breast-bones of naked hens (if they do not bend they have been climbing mountains too long) and to massage their horrid legs. I became very knowing in the fish market, gingerly lifting the gills of the fish to peer into the red horror within (if it is not red it is not fresh) and gazing intently into their glazed eyes, sometimes varnished over with red paint to make them glisten. Then, instructed by Emilia, I would turn disdainfully aside, bid the vendor *adieu*, and inform him over my shoulder that I found nothing worthy of my consideration on his stall that day.

The effect of this little piece of acting is always magical. If Madame plays her part really well, that salesman will suddenly grin and dive *under* his stall. There will follow a frenzied invisible scuffling and spuffling, and he will shortly reappear with a really young and tender chicken or splendid slippery fish caught in the Mediterranean that morning and sometimes gasping still. He will nod his head and wink his eye at Madame, and inform her delightedly—what she knows already— that he keeps a very special store for customers who know what is what.

But all this takes time. All shopping in Provence takes time; and when Emilia regularly informs me on her belated return from market twice a week that, owing to the press of people, she lost the local bus by two minutes (it is never by more or less than two minutes), I can fully sympathise with that white lie.

For marketing here is such fun. In addition to meeting all one's friends and hearing the gossip of every household in the neighbourhood, how this Madame can be tiresome and that Monsieur loves his food, one can see (and hear) LIFE.

What more amusing than to watch the pompous Monsieur Jeannot slip on a piece of banana skin and skid into a heap of oranges, some of which scatter under the stalls and are swiftly prigged by alert urchins, while other marketers roller-skate on the remainder? What a rush to rescue the poor Monsieur Jeannot when he finally comes to rest upon a gigantic pat of butter, leaving the impress of an exasperated stern. Even the discomfited Spaniard, who sells the oranges, and massive Madame Gorini, who vends that butter, join in laughing sympathy as they collect their fruits and scrape and slap the butter back into shape. Everybody — except perhaps Monsieur Jeannot—feels better for an episode such as this.

All peasants have their theatrical instinct, and each tiny incident must always be dramatised and made into a tragedy, comedy, or farce, else life would be but a dull affair.

One day when I was shopping a sudden shriek rent the hot atmosphere of the market-place, and every eye turned towards the *Droguerie* from whence that shriek came. Out into the sunshine burst stout Widow Pin, who owns the shop, gasping for air, clasping her ample tumpkin and

Monsieur Jeannot slips on a banana skin.

rolling her little black eyes. She was seized with a paroxysm of sneezing and coughing, and, as sympathetic friends banged her on the back and flapped their aprons in her face, she gasped out that she has sniffed by mistake a bottle of *Sel Ammoniac* (ammonia), mistaking it for the popular disinfectant *Eau de Javel*.

Consolation was immediately offered in the form of an *apéritif* by Monsieur Jacques, a miserly bachelor, who has had his eye on that *Droguerie* business for years, and evidently thought that the price of that consolatory restorative might in the end prove to be a good investment. After all, the widow is lonely ; she is many years his senior ; and, if he could induce her to marry him, she will almost certainly predecease him, leaving him the proud owner of one of the most prosperous shops in the town. And so that episode closed on a note of hope.

Much as I love marketing, I have realised that if I deprived Emilia of her bi-weekly purchasing expeditions I should probably deprive myself of her services. I find that she gets better prices than I, and, knowing her market inside out and having personal friends at every stall, she gets far better merchandise.

Of course in many cases it is dangerous to leave the marketing to the *bonne*, for she will probably add *centimes* to every purchase marked down in her little note-book and pocket the surplus. But

Emilia does not do that. If she gets little presents and commissions here and there, that is her business and not my affair, for never yet have I detected a higher price noted in her grubby little book.

But although I find it wiser and more politic to leave food-stores to Emilia, I can at least enjoy shopping by myself and with appreciative English friends.

One of these wanted a new pair of bedroom slippers to match her blue dressing-gown. Accordingly we slid together down the steep and narrow streets of the old town, and there, in *Rue Droite* (so called because, like " The Street that was called Straight " in the East, it is the twistiest in the town), she saw in a little window exactly what she wanted.

There, lying beside a neat pair of grey slippers, were the very blue ones she had set forth to find. Entering joyfully, she asked the shopkeeper the price of that blue pair of slippers.

He looked at her doubtfully. The grey pair were far more *chic*, and cheaper, too, he informed her.

Perhaps ; but it was the blue pair she wanted. They matched her *peignoir* exactly. What was their price ?

They were not her size, protested the little man,

but the grey pair would, he was convinced, fit Madame perfectly.

Madame became slightly irritated ; she also became obstinate. She did not want the grey slippers. Surely there would be another blue pair of a larger size in one of the many boxes with which his shelves were piled ?

There might be, said the shopman, shaking his head dubiously, but also—there might not. Now the grey pair of slippers were perfect for Madame, exactly her size, and the colour toned so well with her grey hair.

Why might she not have the slippers she wanted ? demanded Madame in amused exasperation. Would it not be easy to look for another blue pair and so satisfy her ?

No, not easy, she was informed emphatically. It would mean the ascent—perhaps the repeated ascent—of a ladder, the opening, probably with no satisfactory result, of many boxes. The day was hot and he was tired. If Madame would only buy that grey pair of slippers she would certainly be delighted with them, and he would be extremely grateful to her for sparing him the trouble involved in a search for another blue pair. Or, with a sudden flash of inspiration, if Madame would come again in a fortnight's time, he would have had time by then for a thorough search at his leisure.

My friend, overcome by his piteous expression and the Provençal method of salesmanship, thereupon took her departure with me, and we laughed all the way home. The little slipper merchant had not excited our admiration for his business methods, but he had established a bond of human sympathy between the three of us, for we could so perfectly understand his aversion from exerting himself in that heat, and liked him for confessing the real reason for his reluctance.

I think that is the chief charm of living in Provence, the perfectly natural behaviour of the people. They express exactly what they are feeling without shame and without reserve. They are so human and, therefore, so easy to understand, and to love.

The little barber of the town is a great friend of mine. I made his acquaintance in the following manner. My husband having been ill for some time and unable to shave himself, grew restive under his growth of beard, and I, who particularly dislike ' beavers,' suggested driving to the town to collect the local barber and bring him to the bedchamber of Monsieur. This brilliant idea was greeted with enthusiasm, and I accordingly made an appointment and drove forth early next morning to the town.

The little barber was already hopping about on

his doorstep clad in an immaculate white coat
and brushing his new ' Trilby ' hat.

" *Chapeau Anglais!* " he exclaimed proudly,
waving it at me in greeting. He then popped
it on his head at a rakish angle that was entirely
French, picked up the implements of his trade,
the patent mowing-machine, the soap, the strop,
the razor, and the little scissors, which were, of
course, insufficiently wrapped up in a page of
L'Eclaireur de Nice, dropped them all in his excitement, crawled round and under the car, into
the gutter and all over the pavement in search
of them like an excited centipede, thereby tripping
up several respectable citizens and getting himself
thoroughly disliked.

I watched the scene delightedly. Hats were
doffed, apologies made amid a frenzy of staccato
bowing and the sound of nervous laughter, ex-
planations given to the policeman on duty who
came up to expostulate with me for drawing up
my car on the wrong side of the road and remain-
ing for so long in a forbidden position ; and at
last the little barber was packed, complete with
instruments, into my car, and we drove off.

I asked the little man which road he would
prefer to take, and, although various clients were
impatiently awaiting his ministrations in the shop,
he promptly chose the longest route. It was not

every day, he said, that he had the opportunity of a drive in so smart a car, and never before had he been driven by so gracious a lady. He bounced about in his seat excitedly, pointed to objects of interest with an agitated arm stretched dangerously across my eyes, waved salutations proudly to his friends, and generally made himself an amusing nuisance.

Arrived within the Domaine, he suddenly espied Hilaire, recognised him as an old friend, and became so restless that I perforce stopped the car to allow the gesticulating little creature to alight and shake hands with his old comrade.

"*Nous avons fait la guerre ensemble !*" explains Hilaire, working the little barber's arm up and down like a pump-handle. "*Comment ça va, mon vieux ?*"

Realising that Monsieur, upstairs, would be chafing to get rid of "his accursed beard," as he calls it, I curtailed the exchange of inquiries, compliments, and war-time reminiscences and hustled the little barber upstairs.

He plied his scissors and razor with skill and dexterity. It was the preliminaries, the compliments, the removal of the Trilby hat, the mopping of the brow, the admiring exclamations about the house of Monsieur and Madame that took the time. When the ceremony was over and

Monsieur, smooth and beaming, leaned back in his chair with a sigh of content ; when Madame had been fetched to see how beautiful he looked and had received the first unprickly salutation for some weeks (while the little barber discreetly turned his back), she, in her turn, plied the little man with compliments upon his skill, and herself brought him wine and biscuits on a lordly dish before driving him back to face his furious customers waiting in the shop.

On the return drive he assured me that in future he was mine to command for the smallest service, and that if the health of Monsieur should at any time relapse and Madame be anxious, I had only to send a telephone message to the shop, and, when his day's work should be over, he would come and watch by the bed of Monsieur during the nights so that Madame might gain a little repose.

How touching! The little barber, like all Provençaux, has a heart. The toilette of Monsieur took time to accomplish, but how worth while were those two hours.

In the spring, by some mischance, Monsieur dropped and broke his eyeglass. In Provence, where houses have marble or tiled floors in their halls and passages, a dropped eyeglass is almost certainly a broken eyeglass. Cursing softly to himself, he walked to the town and made his way down the tortuous streets to the shop of the optician, where he ordered half a dozen eyeglasses. Returning for them after the promised fortnight, he was told, to his great annoyance, that there had been such pressure of work owing to the imminent *première Communion* that his order had not yet been completed.

"Does everyone wear an eyeglass for that particular service?" he inquired irritably, and was told by the little optician, who was much hurt by the levity of the question, that his little daughter was one of the candidates and that her father and mother had been very much overworked in consequence, preparing her outfit, inviting god-parents and relatives to attend the ceremony and the banquet afterwards. The importance of business in Provence pales before the importance of these family events. In France the family comes even before the amassing of money.

At the feast held by a sister of our Emilia after *la première Communion* of her little niece, every relative brought his or her complete family. A room was hired in a little hotel and decorated at great expense, and one corner of it was hidden by a flower-decked screen to conceal a huge divan, also flower-strewn, on which were piled the babes, new-born and otherwise, of all the invited guests in one glorious squealing heap. Their cries were completely drowned, so Emilia assured me, by the loud-speaker relaying opera from Rome, which was lent by the management, and by the *impromptu* music provided by one and all in turn. At intervals during this repast certain blushing young mothers retired behind the screen to assuage the appetites of their young, and towards morning there was peace as baby after baby fell asleep among the drooping flowers.

But the point was that every single member of that family had been present on the great occasion, coming from distant provinces, leaving their respective jobs to take care of themselves until such time as the family festivities should cease.

Conseils de famille also interrupt business for an indefinite time. We suffer from them frequently. I have never made up my mind as to which is the more shattering to our domestic equilibrium : these family councils or the mourning of our staff. The telephone is a new and useful toy to them, and is monopolised at all hours when some family event is to take place. Emilia sits enthroned on the divan in the hall, wound up in telephone cords and wires, grasping the receiver in both floury (or fishy, or meaty, or vegetabley) hands, puce in the face with excitement, shrieking condolences and counsel, and arranging appointments with one and all of her family at the top of her voice.

I have no wish to eavesdrop, but unless I climbed to the highest peak of the Alps I could hardly avoid overhearing the plans of Emilia and those of her family. The news that we are to lose her immediately —and for several days — while her family affairs or funeral feasts are in train, floats up to me as I try to write in my isolated tower. It is presently confirmed by Emilia herself, who soon is heard climbing up my tower staircase rather like the little engine of the *train Sud* as it puffs and snorts up our mountain gradient.

" Grasping the receiver in floury hands."

Of course I consent to let her go. When we first came to Provence I was inclined to resent these

upheavals of our domestic peace, until a wise
friend who has lived here for years pointed out
to me how well worth while these concessions were,
what happiness they gave, and what devoted service
was given in return.

And so we always resign ourselves with what
patience we can muster to the period of discomfort
that follows upon Emilia's tumultuous departure.
A bereaved and cheerless quiet descends upon the
house until, some days later, she bursts upon us
again without warning (the telephone, it appears,
is only used among her relatives), and the house
is once more flooded with comfort and cheerful
noise. Emilia is back again, her family affairs, for
the moment, settled.

Of course I have to hear all the ins and outs
of whatever affair has been in hand, and I confess
that I enjoy these graphic recitals. On one
occasion Emilia had to attend the Mass arranged
for her family at the end of a period of mourning
for some relative. Oh! the telephonings and the
little journeys into the town and surrounding
country to rope in all the relations, and the difficulty of collecting them all on the same day at the
same hour. One sister had influenza ; the baby
of another was teething and could not be left ;
a brother in the country was picking his olives
with his family ; a cousin had just killed a pig,

" Picking his olives with his family."

and the sausage-man, who visits all outlying
farms and makes hams, sausages, &c., for the
peasants' store, was expected on the suggested

day. The complications were endless ; but at last Emilia, who is an excellent organiser and administrator, managed to fix a date convenient to them all, and returned from her last expedition flushed and somewhat exhausted, but triumphant.

They had chosen 7 A.M. for their Mass because, being early, it was cheaper—half-price, in fact. This meant that Emilia must sleep at home because the local bus to the town did not start early enough. She left an easily arranged meal for us and bustled off in her mourning crape, string bag in hand because after the service she would visit the market and bring back her household stores, so killing two birds with one stone.

She returned next day—Furious.

The whole family—twenty of them—had duly assembled ; her organisation was complete, but alas ! the priest had forgotten all about their special Mass. There they all were, shivering in their best black, for the morning was cold and grey, but no priest.

At length he arrived, too late, and suggested that they should have a later service, and pay a double fee, of course.

Not they ! What an idea !

Hearing the shrill and spirited account of this *contretemps* from the lips of Emilia, I could well imagine the scene and the noise—the voice of

Emilia multiplied by twenty. In the end the priest suggested desperately that the family should attend another special Mass which was being said for another mourning party, and this they did.

But to pay fees to share the flowers and prayers arranged for a man unknown to them had proved the last straw, and Emilia's family had returned to the parental mansion to drink coffee, into which they doubtless poured the bitter gall of their resentment.

Our omelette was very well beaten that morning, and hearing the violence in the kitchen I imagined that Emilia was, in spirit, beating up that negligent priest into a froth.

And so that episode ended, but we have no security that our lives may not again be disturbed, for the Provençal peasant is the most litigious person. He is always suing his neighbour for something—generally about boundaries of property —and on market day the outer office of the lawyer is packed to suffocation with peasants, so bursting with their grievances that their broadcloth positively cracks as they sit waiting their turn to let off steam in the inner sanctuary.

Emilia has quarrelsome brothers, and their father rashly parcelled out his old rambling house between them at his death. Emilia has one floor of the house, and the electric meter is in it. The consumption for the whole house is recorded on this meter, and unless the brothers fork out their share and pay it to her, she is responsible for the complete payment to the company. One can imagine the complications that arise. But she can revenge herself upon the defaulters by pulling out the main plug and plunging the whole house in darkness. However, her brothers inherit the same invincible spirit, and they retaliate promptly by cutting off the water supply of the house, the main being in their portion of it.

Then they all, in turn, visit the lawyer, and war rages until such a time as one or other of them is ill or overtaken by some misfortune, when immediately all petty squabbles are forgotten and the complete family rush and rally round the unfortunate. Electric light floods the house once more and water flows freely from every tap.

I once had occasion to consult a Provençal lawyer. It was about a cheque paid in advance for goods which were not delivered. The man of law promised to write a stringent letter and to produce cheque or goods within the week. Three weeks passed. The lawyer was always engaged six deep whenever I called to see him, and his telephone number was always occupied. And then one day an odd taxi-driver in the town met me by chance in the market, stopped his car, skipped out, and informed me that he had met *Monsieur le Notaire* (my lawyer) in the street a few days before and the lawyer had asked him to tell me—if he chanced to see me—that it would be quite all right about my cheque. So is business conducted in Provence.

Postal business here is also conducted in the same charmingly informal manner. At one time there was a very attractive little lady in charge of one of the lesser Post Offices. Her sleek head, her almond eye, her tinted face, and wicked red mouth proved a great lure to all the males of the town, who found every possible excuse to visit the Post Office. She was extremely efficient, and proved many times a day that it is possible to do several things at the same time. She telephoned telegrams while handing out stamps and making eyes at some man, and frequently she examined the stock of some itinerant vendor of silk stockings or fancy goods whilst conducting her business.

If one were in a hurry it was generally wiser to go elsewhere for postal matter. This lady never neglected hers for a moment, but the *queue* of admirers was long, and unless one visited the Post Office early it meant a long wait. If one had leisure, of course, a visit to that office was better than a play.

But in all Provençal Post Offices the business

is leisurely and interrupted. Not only do petty savings of the peasants take long to deposit, English telegrams an age to telephone, and the payment of telephone accounts, which must be entered, docketed and stamped (the subscriber always paying for the receipt stamp), an interminable time to discharge, but sometimes domestic matters intervene.

Once I had to wait while the Postmaster fixed up a complete funeral of one of his relatives by the telephone on his desk, suggesting that Aunt So-and-So should take the *charabanc* from such-and-such a town to the appointed place ; that Uncle Someone-Else should go by train ; that little Paul should be left at home ; that the funeral should be of *la première classe* (a first-class funeral is fully plumed and decorated), and so on, even to the *menu* for the feast at the end of the morning. When it was all satisfactorily fixed up, the Postmaster gravely asked me what my business was and how best he might serve me. Whilst conducting it, he also gave me many intimate details of the fatal malady which had proved too strong for this deceased relative, and since then he has treated me as though I were a member of his family.

Another day I had to send an English telegram. Entering a small Post Office on the outskirts of a big coastal town, I was greeted cheerfully by a little apple-cheeked woman in the office, who peeped out at me through the aperture in her glass screen. I was, for a wonder, the only other person in the Post Office.

I asked for a telegraph form ; the Postmistress supplied one, saw me comfortably settled at a small table pulling whiskers out of the only cross-nibbed pen before dipping it into a small bottle of purple mud, and then addressed me.

She could see that Madame had a good heart, and therefore she was emboldened to ask if Madame would mind being left alone to write her telegram ? Madame Carron, over the way, was expecting the arrival of her first baby at any moment, and she (the Postmistress) felt that the poor woman needed encouragement. A little visit would not take long. If Madame happened to finish writing her telegram before the Postmistress returned—well ! there was a comfortable stove to warm the feet and plenty to read. A hand was swept out in comprehensive gesture, which included the Telephone Directory, various posters explaining the advantage of in-suring against hail, fire, theft, and other thrilling literature.

Madame, of course, nodded assent. Fortunately my telegram was not very urgent, and I also became curious to know if Madame Carron

had drawn a son or a daughter in the **great**
lottery.

The little Postmistress came out from behind
her screen, trotted across the office and out of
the door, which she carefully locked after her for
fear of thieves. I felt that it was a great tribute
to the honesty of my countenance to be locked
in alone with the till, the money orders, the postage
stamps, and a mass of official documents.

After twenty minutes — and it took nearly
that to persuade the vile pen to make legible
signs on the fourth telegraph form after three
had already been spoiled—back came the Postmistress.

She entered in a great bustle. The baby had
not yet arrived, but the midwife had hopes and
the doctor had been sent for. Had it not been
for her devotion to duty—duty must always come
before everything if one held an official position—
the Postmistress would certainly have waited for
the *dénouement*.

She then took my telegram, and, as a reward
for my patience and my good heart, the word
Angleterre was knocked off from the text, thus
saving me two francs fifty centimes. Moreover I
gained yet another friend.

Since then, when I chance to enter that Post
Office, I am always given news of the little daughter

of Madame Carron and am treated almost as an honorary godmother.

So, at the price of a little patience and time, does one amass friends in this lovely land ; and, as I have long since learned that life is the fuller of joys because the fuller of friends, I consider myself a rich and happy woman, in spite of the broken £ sterling.

To attempt to speed things up in Provence is but a further waste of time and energy. It is exactly like trying to swim in warm mud. Better far just to wallow cosily in it. To change the ways of the Provençaux one would be obliged to change their character and climate—both impossibilities— and I, for one, should hate to do either, even had I the power.

HOUSEKEEPING.

AFTER the war, when 'Ichabod' was writ large
on the lintels of all the greater houses, the glory
of a well-trained staff of servants under a com-
petent housekeeper had departed, and, with the
increase of taxation, came everywhere the corresponding decrease of staff.

Our household contracted every year until, in
our little labour-saving house in Hertfordshire,
we reached what I thought to be the minimum—
only a married couple.

But when we came to Provence, and the £
sterling collapsed, I found that we could do still
better. It is considered mere 'swank' for two
people with a reduced income to need more than
a *bonne-à-tout-faire* to look after them. *Tant
mieux*, only one extra mouth to feed and only
one pair of hands to break the crockery. And
there is still one further reduction we can make ;
Madame herself can become the *bonne-à-tout-faire*
if conditions do not improve. But to begin with
we would start with a *bonne*, preferably Italian,
because Italians have more heart, and I do like
my servants to be kind to me.

We began badly in a hired flat belonging to kind English people, who stocked our larder before our arrival, and provided a *bonne*, whom we found already installed. She had once been excellent, but had grown lazy and avaricious, and for one interminable month we suffered much from Marthe.

Of course I knew nothing of housekeeping in Provence ; the queer measures and weights, the house-cleaning apparatus and methods, the prices in the market, or the best local shops. So Marthe ' did ' for us, and, to use a colloquialism, ' did us brown.' Even though vegetables out here are always cooked in butter in the better-class houses, I found 8 kilos per week (more than 16 lb. in English weight) somewhat excessive for a household of three. But Marthe was a good business woman, and, having a little flat of her own in the town, wisely, perhaps, laid up a store for her own winter use when our building at the little Domaine should be finished and her temporary job with us over.

She was a noisy woman, Marthe, and all her exits and her entrances were heralded by a CRASH. There were glass communicating doors between the rooms, and these gave her excellent scope. When her hands were full she would hook a stumpy leg, clad in a darned, black stocking, round these doors to close them. The only thing I missed with regret, when Marthe made her final shattering exit, was that stumpy leg, which could always hook a smile out of me.

She was succeeded by Jeanne — a lovely little Bretonne, whom *Madame* engaged because of her beautiful blue-black head and deep violet eyes, and *Monsieur* because of her extraordinarily tiny feet. Happily there were brains in that head, and the tiny feet in their purple *pantoufles* pattered about very willingly, and, thank God, noiselessly, in our service. Jeanne was an excellent cook, and economical. Delicious *soufflés* and *omelettes* did her ridiculously small hands whip

" Hook a stumpy leg . . . round these doors to close them."

up in a trice. But, as I always feared, she was far too attractive to be allowed to stay with us for ever, as we had hoped. When she returned from her ' day out,' always she appeared with her arms full of lovely hot-house flowers or fruits, gifts, as she informed *Madame* with a tell-tale blush, from her *friends* in Cannes. But *Madame* was not deceived by the plural number; and when a telegram arrived one day summoning Jeanne to the sick-bed of a sister, my terrible instinct told me that it had been sent from Cannes by a lover impatient of the sixteen kilometres and the many domestic duties which separated him from those wonderful violet eyes.

Anyhow, Jeanne, white-faced and tearful, for we had been very happy together, said good-bye to us, promising to return as soon as she could. But, of course, she never did.

Her substitute, ridiculously named Pierrette, and found in a hurry, was exactly like a whale. The same small fishy eyes, the same enormous bulk. When she bent down to search for something in the sideboard cupboard, it was completely obscured by her gigantic *derrière*. She rolled from room to room, and complained to me that her bed was too small and that she rolled out of it on to the floor. Of course she did. What single bed could have contained that amorphous mass of flesh ? But she was a magnificent cook (and perhaps this accounted for her acreage), though she nauseated me when she suggested succulent dishes by licking her loose lips between her sentences as though already savouring choice morsels of the delicacies she meant to prepare.

She was also a noisome snob. In Provence, thank heaven, titles mean less than nothing. Everyone is called *Monsieur* or *Madame*, and if nice, is liked and respected ; if nasty, ignored. But Pierrette came from Northern France, and had, moreover, been demoralised by seasonal jobs with rich Americans and English on the Riviera coast, and so had learned the spurious value of a title. When she discovered ours, she came swimming into my bedroom with sycophantic hands outspread and asked me if it were really true that we were ' *noble*.' She had heard it from the fishmonger, and seemed to doubt this fishy source of information. I tried to translate the " kind hearts are more than coronets . . ." platitude into French, but the mischief was done. Pierrette expressed herself *enchantée* to find herself in our service, &c. But *Madame*, in future, must not soil her noble hands with housework ; she, Pierrette, hitherto an arch-shirk, must henceforth do it all. A most disgusting conversation. *Madame* then and there decided that she preferred soiling her hands with any filthy job to enduring longer the close proximity of that poisonous Pierrette.

But next time the gods were really kind to us.

They sent us Emilia. She had been described to me as *très travailleuse, dévouée, et dégourdie,* and we were to find her all three—and more besides. The moment she stepped briskly into the room to be interviewed I felt reassured. That firm square little body in its neat black dress looked healthy and active. I liked her good square jaw, the clear olive skin flushed with a warm carnation tint, and those merry black eyes twinkling at me so humorously.

I warned her that, if she came to us, for several months there would be very hard work and probably great discomfort, with vans of furniture arriving from England to be put into a house only half-built. I told her that we might have to camp uncomfortably in the unfinished house— in the winter, too. She listened attentively, twinkling all the time, occasionally tucking an errant curl under her hat and pleating up her dress with restless fingers, which seemed itching to be dealing at once with the chaotic conditions I tried to describe.

But when my jeremiad ceased, she merely threw back her head and assured me that she would like to come, and that we were certain always to find something to laugh at ! This was the *bonne* for me, and so the arrangement was made, and Emilia skipped out of the door into the night leaving a light-hearted *Monsieur* and *Madame* behind her.

When Emilia came to us she took me in hand at once : I must be taught to market in the true Provençal style. She was far too tactful to tell me this, but suggested merrily that it might amuse *Madame* to see the market, and the prices. So we set forth together, I with a big basket and she with a capacious string bag. I was informed that the upper market was far more expensive, because most of the English and American visitors were too lazy to slip and slide down the precipitous streets of the old town to the larger market down below. The *marchands* in the upper market had, of course, realised this, and visitors were made to pay for their sloth. Emilia and I naturally descended to the lower market through streets so narrow that lovers in opposite houses could snatch a kiss across them.

Emilia, though Italian, had been born in the town, and it soon appeared that she knew everyone and that everyone knew her. Our descent was interrupted every two minutes by introductions and handshaking, till at last we reached the big market. Not so picturesque as the upper market with its huge plashing fountain and spreading plane-trees, but nevertheless attractive and noisy to a glorious degree ; masses of stalls of varied edible merchandise ranged under one vast iron tent.

" *Snatch a kiss across.*"

I was introduced to all Emilia's special friends, and our marketing took a very long time, but I spent the morning of my life with her, made many charming acquaintances and learned many valuable shopping hints. (*Monsieur*, on my return home, was so jealous that next market day he insisted upon accompanying Emilia and me. He had an enormous success with all her friends, and has since carried on a tremendous flirtation with Madame Morini, the fat and handsome vendor of butter and eggs.)

But on this first day Emilia was in her glory because *Madame* drove her down to the market in her little car—more important though surely less interesting and amusing than packing with a crowd of *bonnes* and their bags and baskets into the smelly local 'bus.

Our car was highly perfumed, too, with onions, Parmesan cheese, fish, and ripe fruits; but our atmosphere lacked the pungent aroma of human exertion as an ingredient, and for this I was thankful.

Arrived at the Domaine after her marketing, Emilia peels off an outer covering (generally in the larder, but with the door open), dons a mauve overall, hurriedly prepares her vegetables, puts them on the fire to cook, and then proceeds to do the housework. This is, apparently, an amusing game. She rushes from room to room with a long T-shaped instrument, over which a damp cloth is tied, rubbing over the corridor tiles. Then she swirls a broom dangerously round the furniture and pokes it into corners. Mats are seized, rushed out-of-doors, given one vigorous Italian kick and bang, and then replaced. A duster is flicked over tables and ornaments, displacing the dust to other tables and ornaments. *Madame* follows surreptitiously in her wake with a small hand-brush and dustpan and a damp duster—English methods and implements despised by Emilia, who, when first recommended to use them, merely tossed her buzzle head, laughed indulgently—and proceeded to work in her own way.

Cleaning silver is the most interesting of all household duties in Provence. A large table is moved into the garden. On it is placed the silver to be cleaned, a kilo (2 lb.) of *Blanc d'Espagne* (whitening), and a litre of *Alcool à Brûler* (methylated spirit). A thick white mud is made with the two ingredients and plastered over the silver with a sticky rag. The objects are then plunged into tepid water and scrubbed with an enormous kitchen scrubbing-brush (used also for cleaning floors), and are finally dried on an apron, an ovencloth, an old stocking—anything but the cloths and chamois leathers supplied by an anguished mistress for the purpose of drying and polishing silver. The silver-cleaner herself is white to the hair with *Blanc d'Espagne*. Emilia's buzzle head is generally powdered with it, her eyelashes are thick with it, her overall coated with it, and our dining-room carpet afterwards bears the white footprints of two fat little feet which have also paddled in the powder lavishly spilt on the ground. It does not surprise me when next I get her list of household necessaries which are lacking, to find the items *Blanc d'Espagne* and *Alcool à Brûler* at the head of it. But I am rather surprised that only one *kilo* of the one and one *litre* of the other were used for that silver-cleaning.

And the silver, of course, looks far worse than it did before, save that the design is enriched by a pattern of five—or maybe ten—pudgy fingermarks outlined in white powder on its smeared

surface. But Emilia, bless her, has had a really
enjoyable afternoon.

She is proud of the contents of the Domaine,
and boasts of them far and wide. So loudly did
she boast to old Hilaire, our gardener, that, when
occasionally he is left to caretake during her
holiday, he sleeps—or rather wakes—with a large

" Sleeps with a large shot-gun by his side . . . in case of voleurs.*"*

shot-gun by his side to fire into the air in case of
voleurs who might break in and steal the possessions
of *Monsieur* and *Madame*, which, after all, are
nothing so very wonderful. The poor old thing
told me, innocently, that he liked hearing our old
English grandfather clock striking hour after hour
till dawn ; and from this I gathered that he was

far too scared to sleep. So I told him that the telephone in the hall was a far better companion to a lonely watcher, who could, in case of need, summon aid at any hour of the night from the town. This had not occurred to him, and his old face brightened. Could *Madame* explain to him how the machine worked ? *Madame* did. She even drove into the town and rang him up from a shop, and devoutly wished she had not, since his answering roar nearly broke her ear-drum. But after that, Hilaire never felt nervous again.

When the enlargement of our house was at last finished, we realised that Emilia must have help of some sort. And as the various *femmes de ménage* (the Provençal equivalent of the English ' char ') always failed, sooner or later, through some domestic crisis, to appear on the day appointed, we decided to get a young girl to ' live in.' It seemed an extravagance, but if I were to continue to polish baths and make beds (though I place myself second to none in both these exciting sports) I should never have time for any writing ; and this my husband was kind enough to think would be a pity. Therefore Marie, aged sixteen, was engaged.

Marie was a young Italian elephant, beautiful to look upon but clumsy and unclean. In vain did I buy her new black overalls and white aprons wherewith to clothe her generous limbs before waiting at table. She never looked anything but a slut.

Her 'star' entrance into the dining-room was when my brother-in-law was staying with us. I arranged the dinner-table myself, and it looked very dainty with its fresh linen and bowl of floating roses. I particularly enjoined Marie to wash her face and brush her hair, and, knowing that she had a new outfit for service at meals, I felt fairly confident that her appearance would pass muster.

Imagine my horror when she appeared in the filthiest black overall, with sleeves rolled up, displaying, certainly, very comely brown arms ; a stained and crumpled muslin apron, bare legs, and muddy *pantoufles* (felt bedroom slippers). Her handsome little face had, it is true, been washed, and Emilia assured me afterwards that she had brushed the hair of *la petite* herself. But both of them had ignored the attempt at a middle parting, which zigzagged across her head like forked lightning.

When she had served the little cups of soup, I excused myself and shot into the kitchen to inquire into this scandal. Yes, Marie *was* wearing her new overall and apron, but had been helping Emilia to wash and trim the vegetables at the great *bassin* (water-tank) at the top of the garden.

Why not wash them in the new porcelain kitchen sink? And why not do the washing of vegetables before putting on the new service outfit that I had provided?

Why not, indeed! But both Emilia and Marie regarded me with liquid reproachful eyes as though *I* were the eccentric and unreasonable person.

I went back to the dining-room and resumed my seat. Marie presently appeared arrayed in her clean pink print overall provided for rough work in the house. Hopeless. But at least she looked clean.

Marie was also a Destroyer. Only a capital D could adequately express my feelings each time Emilia—never the culprit herself—came to confess to me some new breakage.

Marie also, as the hot weather advanced, became whiffy. And when we finally dismissed her, and her empty room was prepared for her successor, I discovered, not to my surprise, that her toilet jug and basin were still stuffed with packing-straw, and had therefore never once been used since our furniture and effects had come from England some months before. The house was sweeter and safer for the departure of Marie.

Lucienne, who came after her, is a handsome hard-faced French girl: tremendously capable, tremendously alive to the main chance, but not a lovable personality like Emilia. But she is quick, hard-working, honest, and clever, and has a sense of humour in which I delight.

Old Hilaire predicted war to the knife when he heard that we had engaged a Frenchwoman to work with the Italian Emilia. But, quite astonishingly, he was proved wrong, for they get on famously together. Perhaps because Emilia, discovering that Lucienne has a hard-hearted mother and has never known tenderness, at once adopted Lucienne as her own special care, and lavishes her superabundant store of maternal kindness upon her. There is but five years' interval between their ages, but that makes no difference to Emilia, who always alludes to Lucienne as ' *ma petite.*'

It is a sight to see them washing the flannels in the downstairs bathroom, which, the moment it was finished and fully equipped for the use of guests, was prigged at once by Emilia and Lucienne as a *lavoir*. They sit side by side on little stools above the bath foaming to its brim with soapy water. ('Lux' soap diamonds are such fun to play with, and, if you use two or three packets for one bath, you get the loveliest slimy froth. And, after all, it is *Madame* who pays for them.) I hear shrieks of laughter issuing from within. The buzzle head of Emilia, crowned with soap-spume playfully laid upon it by Lucienne, who compares it to a cream bun, peeps through the scarlet geraniums that frame the little window. Lucienne's sharp French nose is decorated at the tip with a soap-sud. They tell me that they are driving their automobile as they sit and pound and rub and wring the flannels side by side. Thus

Washing in the bath.

they turn a tiresome job into a game, and it is ever thus with them.

Jam-making is, however, their greatest sport. When the harvest of orange-blossom is plucked and the wild oranges turn golden, everyone picks them for *confiture d'oranges*, a delicious bitter marmalade.

Neighbours this year vied with each other in showering these wild oranges upon us until Emilia, grown desperate, announced her intention of making marmalade at once. From that moment everything in the house became sticky. Emilia and Lucienne were up to the eyes in marmalade. The kitchen table and all that was laid thereon became coated with it. Forks, spoons, and knives stuck to our hands ; plates clung to the table-cloth. The smell of cooking oranges pervaded the whole house ; every casserole and kitchen vessel was filled with soaking oranges ; the stove completely covered with preserving pans, some of them borrowed from an obliging American neighbour. Even our *lingerie* was stiffened with marmalade after the sticky hands of Lucienne had ironed and folded it ; for in Provence the maids do all the household ironing as part of their job.

When a mass of pots were filled and I had soaked papers in brandy to preserve the marmalade, and we had tied on the covers and labelled the jars, Emilia proudly invited *Monsieur* to enter her ' jam-shop.' When he made his enthusiastic exit, his feet stuck to the parquet in his study. He had been paddling in marmalade.

The cherry season is even funnier ; for when the stones are all taken out of the fruit preparatory to making jam, our two maidens are stained crimson all over. Emilia dramatically informs me that she and Lucienne are murderers, and that their victim is stewing in the preserving pan.

But, though a messy occupation, the resulting jam is quite excellent, and the jam-makers have had great fun.

That is the joy of Provençal servants; they are so joyous. They may lack method; they may often be slovenly in their ways—they generally are—but they work like little willing slaves from early morning till night, and they never sulk. They may have volcanic outbursts of temper, but, as they always express what they feel at the moment, they get rid of the thing fermenting within their minds and hearts in one explosion, instead of letting it turn sour within them. And they are so perfectly natural that one cannot take offence or be shocked when they do unconventional things.

For instance, a friend of mine drove with her chauffeur into Italy. As they crossed the frontier the sun rose and the day became hot. Jean (her chauffeur) removed his cap and drove with his curls flying. Later he also removed his chauffeur's tunic. My friend noted that occupants of passing cars fixed a fleeting scandalised gaze upon Jean. But when she stopped for a picnic luncheon and remarked that his shirt was unbuttoned to the waist, displaying a hairy chest, she ceased to wonder—or rather she wondered only whether the farther they progressed into Italy the less

Jean would have on, until at last he would achieve a state of nature.

In the state of comfortable *déshabille* described, he served the *al fresco* luncheon of *Madame la Comtesse*, and then sat down by her side and entertained her with naïve courtesy. I am glad to say that she had not the heart to reprove him.

On another occasion, when driving her through the wet darkness of a stormy night, he suddenly drew up the car, alighted, and, much to her concern, vanished. She imagined herself to be abandoned in the lonely mountains, at that time not knowing well her Jean, who was newly engaged. After some time he, to her immense relief, reappeared, pushed a beaming face into the window of the car, and observed confidentially : " *Je ne pouvais plus me tenir.*"

But they have humour and they have heart, these children of nature. If one can only make some unpalatable criticism in an amusing way, they laugh and remember. If one considers them, they repay each tiny act of kindness by warm-hearted and devoted service.

And how delicious are their touches of romance and sentimentality ! Will *Monsieur* or *Madame* ever forget that pair of pigeons, roasted, heads and all, with a white blossom in the beak of each and the beaks touching, that Emilia dished up on their wedding anniversary, the nearest approach to turtle-doves that she could find ?

Or the great bouquet of white carnations purchased with the scanty *sous* of Emilia and Lucienne and presented to *Madame* when she donned, as is her custom, her wedding-dress and veil on that occasion to dine with *Monsieur* ?

When *Monsieur* was seriously ill, it was beautiful to see how both devoted little maids resolutely

" Roasted, heads and all."

refused to take even one afternoon off duty until the danger was past; how, every day, they each paid a tiptoe visit to the door of that sick-room to whisper: *" Courage ! Monsieur ! Courage toujours ! "* descending afterwards to the kitchen with swimming eyes. How they vied with each other when he became convalescent in running errands for him, and how they blew kisses to his unconscious back when at last he was able to take his first walk.

These are the things that really matter in life. These are the things that *Madame* will always remember in her heart.

OFFICIALDOM.

Hot sleepy sunshine bathing the little square in front of the Mairie. A mongrel cur dozing upon the baked hot paving-stones, scratching himself at intervals, then grunting and changing his position. In the shade of the cathedral on the other side of the square a toothless old woman sits huddled together, mumbling and mouthing silently as she fingers her rosary. Only a handful of children, skipping about on hard little brown feet, chasing each other in and out of archways which look like drowsy gaping mouths, seem unaffected by the torrid heat.

I was much affected by it. I hate heat, but stern necessity had brought me down to the Mairie on official business at this early hour of an August afternoon. We had received a mysterious paper informing us that we must be taxed upon two properties, whereas we possessed but one. A notice had appeared in the local newspaper informing tax-payers that the *Percepteur*, who deals with these matters of finance, would be in his office at the Mairie on each successive day

" Hot sleepy sunshine bathing the little square."

after a certain date to answer inquiries, redress wrongs, and so forth.

I had descended our mountain to seek an

audience with the *Percepteur*, leaving my husband to his siesta. The French of *Monsieur* was much too pure and good ever to be understood in Provence. Also his natural dignity was far too great to allow the aid and relief of violent gesticulation. *Madame*, with her knowledge of dancing and her flow of *argot* (slang), is always comprehensible to the Provençaux, and therefore it is always she who conducts the business.

Today I had come down to the Mairie armed with various papers and resigned to a long and eloquent conversation with the *Percepteur*.

A *gendarme* was leaning against the door-post of the police station, which is just under the central arch of the Mairie. His tunic and shirt were unbuttoned, revealing a hairy chest, and he was smoking a Caporal cigarette and reading a newspaper. I recognised in him a friend who had once come to my rescue when I had cleverly shut myself out of my own car. I had carefully locked all the windows and one of the doors from the inside and then slammed the driver's door, forgetting that the handle had been broken off in a slight collision with a wall. This gentleman, now in *déshabille*, had been on point duty at the time, and, leaving the traffic to take care of itself, had tried with every implement in his pocket to force that lock. It was pouring with rain at the time, yet we, and the crowd that inevitably assembles on these occasions, had managed to extract a vast amount of amusement from my predicament.

Hearing footsteps, my *gendarme* looked over his news-sheet, and when he saw me, his whole face split up into a grin. Then he dropped his newspaper and hastily began to fasten his tunic as he asked me if he could be of any service. Perhaps my car was again *en panne* (in trouble) he suggested slyly. I laughingly reassured him and inquired where was the office of *Monsieur le Percepteur*, and he told me that it was on the fifth floor.

I groaned and threw up my eyes. He chuckled sympathetically, and acted a little pantomime to express his opinion that the day was too hot, and that he was thankful it was I and not he who needs must mount that great stone stairway to the fifth floor.

I mounted it in a very leisurely manner, meeting and greeting more acquaintances among the *gendarmerie* upon every landing. At length I reached the fifth floor, and there, upon the door of the *Percepteur*, marked with his name in huge painted capitals, I saw an oblong white notice with the word *FERMÉ* scrawled upon it in drunken capitals.

Closed ! After all my trouble in coming three broiling kilometres to consult the great man. I was certain that I had not misread that notice in the newspaper, but, to make quite sure, I descended those five flights of stairs to consult the news-sheet of my friend in the doorway.

I was quite right. The *Percepteur* had invited all those who were in trouble to come to him for comfort and counsel between the hours of two and four o'clock each day of that particular week. My friend the *gendarme* could not account for the absence of the *Percepteur*, but he would in-quire within. He vanished, and presently returned with two comrades, the older and fatter of whom tapped his nose roguishly and whispered

Door Fermé.

to me that he had seen *Monsieur le Percepteur* go up those stairs an hour ago—and he had not since descended them.

When I looked blank, spoke of the notice *FERMÉ* hung upon the door, he gave a roar of laughter, shook his head knowingly and said :

" *Il faut insister, Madame !* "

Oh ! so that was it. That old fox of a *Percepteur* had gone to earth up there, had he ? Doubtless he was enjoying a nice siesta instead of attending to his business. Very well, I would return and I certainly would 'insist.'

Insist I did. I walked up and down that corridor

beating a tattoo upon every door in it at discreet intervals, with a final bombardment upon the door marked *PERCEPTEUR*, for twenty minutes by the Mairie clock.

Not a sound came from within (and I was listening now and again for a snore), but I had grown 'cussed' as is my wont when I

" Percepteur *had gone to earth*."

encounter obstacles. Knowing that that old man was somewhere behind those locked doors, I continued to tap, and was unshaken in my determination to go on tapping until one or other of those doors was opened. Or else I would sit on one of the benches that lined the corridor and wait until *Monsieur le Percepteur* grew hungry and emerged for his supper.

With enough patience and the saving gift of humour one can generally obtain all that one desires in Provence.

My persistence was rewarded at last, and suddenly there was a brisk turning of a key in a lock, the door of *Monsieur le Percepteur* shot open, and in the doorway stood a charming old man in a black velvet skull-cap smiling at me ingratiatingly with an air of innocent surprise.

" *Monsieur le Percepteur ?* " I asked.

" *Mais oui, Madame, Entrez-donc !* " was the hearty reply, and he ushered me into his office. No word of reproof or annoyance crossed my lips, nor of regret, apology or explanation his, though I could not resist one expressive glance at the dent in a cushioned arm-chair, the empty coffee-cup on the floor beside it, and the newspaper (in which his own welcoming notice appeared) that had evidently been thrown pettishly aside as *Madame* continued to insist upon admittance.

He caught my eye, raised an eyebrow and chuckled—that was all. We understood each other perfectly.

Then we proceeded to business and cleared up the little misunderstanding. Our small garage had been taxed as an additional property and

taxed higher than the house and garden put together. The *Percepteur* explained to me that in
Provence a garage was considered to be a luxury,
whereas a house was a necessity. So I paid for
my two properties and departed.

Later in the year I had yet another experience of the same type in the same building. I
had taken down our forms for the renewal of
our *cartes d'identité*—new duplicate photographs,
money, and so on, and had been asked to return
for the books at the end of the month before six
o'clock in the evening.

I obeyed my instructions to the letter, only to
find that particular office closed. Again I inquired
of the police, and was told that the officer in charge
had gone to drink an *apéritif* with a friend, but
would return before the official closing hour if I
would have the goodness to wait.

I explained that *Monsieur* was ill at home, and
that I could not leave him for long, whereupon
three of my kind policemen instantly invaded the
deserted office and began a search for our *cartes
d'identité*. Nowhere could they be found, until a
burly sergeant suddenly guessed that they were
in a locked drawer of a certain table.

In a moment all three men were trying to pick
that lock with every available instrument from a
penknife to a poker, and eventually my fat

sergeant proved successful with the aid of a kitchen fork borrowed from a neighbour in the square, and I was triumphantly handed our *cartes d'identité*.

When we first came to Provence I had asked one of the policemen of our town if the police had some Orphanage Fund to which we could subscribe, as in England we always supported that charity. I was joyfully enrolled as a member of the *Amicale* of the police, and, when given my card of membership, was informed that it would protect me from all annoyances from the police, and that in future it would be safe for me to leave my car in prohibited places, to drive down one-way streets in the wrong direction, and that if a strange *gendarme* should happen to reprove me or accost me, all that I need do was to produce my *Amicale* card and all would be well. In France no one is expected to await the reward of philanthropy in another and a better world. Nothing for nothing and something for something is expected immediately.

" Fat sergeant proved successful with the aid of a kitchen fork."

There is a delightful system of village policemen in Provence. Each hamlet in the mountains has its own pet policeman. He is called the *Garde*, wears a green uniform entirely different from that of the town police, and is the father of the village. If a peasant beats his wife, the *Garde* descends to make peace. If one forgets to renew a dog or car licence, the *Garde* pays a little friendly visit. If the warning is not heeded perhaps a second will be given in a firmer tone, and then, if the repeated admonition is ignored, the *Garde* will report the matter to the police of the nearest town, who deal summarily with the offender. The *Garde* is really a peacemaker rather than a policeman.

Our *Garde* is a darling. He is deliciously rotund and there are gaping voids between the buttons of his over-stretched tunic. He rolls round on his duties and his fat laugh can always be heard a kilometre ahead of him. He has little round black eyes that snap and twinkle and surely see everything, though on occasion they can be conveniently blind. He adores his job, the gossip it provides, and the intimate knowledge of everyone's affairs.

At first I felt nervous when I saw him rolling up our drive, and racked my brains rapidly to remember something I had done that I ought not to have done—or *vice versa*. But I soon learned that, impelled by an insatiable curiosity, he was only having a sniff round, and that his visits always coincided with the arrival of a guest to the Domaine, or just after a *camion* (lorry) had disgorged its load at our house. Satisfied as to the rank and sex of the visitor and the duration of his or her visit, or having found out the contents of that *camion*, he would drink a glass of wine with the cook, pinch the ear of the saucy *femme-de-chambre*, compliment old Hilaire upon his fruit and vegetables, and be given a fat peach or a pocketful of tomatoes by *Madame*, who is proud of her garden, salute her, and roll off elsewhere in quest of further news.

Only once did I call upon his protection as a policeman. It was before our little Domaine was surrounded by a grillage and locked gates. A young maid of ours had gone outside the kitchen to empty some scraps into the chicken-pail, when Emilia heard a shout, a scuffle, and a wild scream from Marie, who fled back into the kitchen white and shaking with terror saying that a man had jumped out at her from the shadows. Emilia dashed into the *Galerie* where *Monsieur* was quietly reading aloud to me, as was his invariable and beautiful custom while I did needlework ; and she poured forth this startling news in a highly dramatic manner. She was convinced that it was a thief who had come to rob our house.

I assured her that a thief would have lain hidden until the household had retired for the night, and certainly would not have betrayed himself by jumping out at Marie and proclaiming his presence by a loud yell. However, I seized an electric torch and rushed out into the garden in pursuit of this mysterious man, and, though I caught no glimpse of him, I did hear the sound of feet scudding down the hill through the olive groves.

Next morning I informed the *Garde* of the adventure, and he was of opinion that the intruder had merely lost himself among the olive groves and, seeing a lighted house, had crept up to it. Then, being startled by the sudden apparition of Marie close to him, he had evidently yelled at her in self-preservation to scare her away while he escaped off private property.

However, that night the *Garde*, bolstered up by the support of two unofficial comrades, took up his station among the olive groves to lie hidden and watch the Domaine. Seeing nothing after an hour or two, and doubtless feeling cold, they all sought the hospitable shelter of our kitchen, where they caroused with our two delighted maidens until midnight.

Next morning the maidens overslept themselves, breakfast was very late, and *Monsieur* much annoyed, also I had to order another *bidon*

146

of *vin ordinaire* (the little wine of the country), and another *kilo* of coffee for the kitchen.

So ended our adventure. Personally I have always thought that the *Garde* was even more scared than Marie. But all the same, though he may lack courage he makes up for it in charm.

I have another visit to the Mairie looming ahead of me. The main roads of Provence are marvellous, smooth as billiard tables, with a perfect camber, and all are triumphs of engineering. The by-roads are by-words. Our Domaine lies at the end of one of them. It begins well, branching off from the main road to Nice, and descending gallantly in wide, sweeping curves to the back gates of an important *Château*—there is snobbery even in road-building.

Beyond the *Château* our by-road deteriorates into a moraine, and a moraine, as I was taught at school, is the rocky bed of a defunct glacier. Our moraine winds round the mountain, along precipitous terraces, to the gates of Domaine de Fort Escu. We are the anticlimax at the end of *Chemin de Malbosc*.

Even so, our moraine is the property of the Mairie and we pay taxes for its upkeep. Upkeep is the right word, for at intervals the supporting wall of a terrace subsides and part of our road rolls down the mountain. Then, as the Mayor seems to have caught the somnolent habits of the *Percepteur* and others who shelter beneath the roof of the Mairie, and nothing is done in the way of swift repair, the various peasants who live in the mountains below our road steal forth at night and filch the great grey boulders, with which the walls are made, and use them for their own purposes. Our giant brigand neighbour has built himself a really fine wall, at least three metres high, to shelter his vines from the Levant wind. Hilaire, who knows all the little ways of the peasants (having doubtless emulated them himself many times in his life), now rushes forth the moment *Madame* reports the collapse of a wall and swiftly repairs the damage before the fallen boulders are bagged by someone ; feeling that it is fruitless to wait for the Mairie to send their own men to do their own work. He has an affection for his *Madame*, English and therefore mad though she may be, and he is determined that she and her car shall come to no harm.

Perhaps the Mayor is a subtle man, knows this fact, and finds it cheaper to leave the work for Hilaire to perform. Anyhow, his attitude is one of glorious indifference to complaints.

Some months ago we were completely isolated from the world by the collapse of a huge wall which entirely blocked our road. Hilaire came to me in a state of wild agitation. He informed me that if I would give him the services of one man for ten days, they would first clear the road and then rebuild the wall. I consented, and he found a worker.

" *L'homme*," as he called his man, was a queer, silent individual, tall and thin, with the longest and baggiest corduroy trousers I ever saw, particularly in the region of the stern. Perhaps the trousers of road-menders are peculiarly constructed to allow ample and safe space for bending. In repose, the trousers of ' *L'homme* ' were hitched so high that they formed a sort of combination suit ; in action they were allowed to slide several degrees lower to give freedom of movement. Upon his bullet head he wore a black felt clerical ' wide - awake ' hat, evidently given to him by some kind English chaplain in the misty past. Decorated on one side with a *panache* of three Italian cheroots with green and scarlet bands, and a lesser frill of Caporal cigarettes stuck into the ribbon which surrounded the crown, that clerical hat assumed a secular air and gave an extraordinary finish to the *toilette* of ' *L'homme*.'

Hilaire was as proud of this first workman he had ever had to work under him as though he had hatched ' *L'homme* ' himself from some gigantic egg. When I attempted amiable conversation with '*L'homme*' and was met with silence and a blank stare, Hilaire whispered triumphantly to me that '*L'homme*' was deaf, as though deafness were a clever accomplishment instead of a misfortune.

However, together they performed prodigies of valour and endurance—for the weather was vile during the whole ten days—and they rebuilt that wall a metre thick and fifteen metres long.

Nevertheless, the time has come when I must form a deputation of indignant neighbours (the chief difficulty will be to whip them up into a proper state of indignation) and call upon the Mayor in person with our joint complaint of *Chemin de Malbosc*, and I have promised Hilaire that he shall bring up the rear of the procession carrying two ruined motor tyres, split and burst by the stones of our moraine, as proof positive that our complaint is not like our road, without foundations.

But will the Mayor be at home upon the day appointed for the personal hearing of complaints ? I trow not, for deputations can prove somewhat exhausting. During the last I heard of, two belligerent neighbours, an old Frenchwoman and an Italian proprietor, actually fell upon each other tooth and claw in the presence of the Mayor, and had to be torn apart by *gendarmes* of the police, hurriedly summoned from the floor below to separate the combatants. I believe it was a question of a boundary.

After this, the deputation was hustled outside the audience chamber, its doors were locked, and a sergeant of police was posted outside them.

At the same time as the collapse of the big wall flanking *Chemin de Malbosc*, the telephone went dumb. This happened after one of the torrential November rains, when tiny streams become torrents, overflow their banks, and come cascading and crashing down the mountains, bursting through every aperture and crevice in road or wall, and the air is full of the sound of many waters. The final thunder-storm, when rivers of blue lightning rushed down the lightning-conductor of my tower, and hailstones as big as robins' eggs tore and smashed my flowers and vegetables to ribbons and pulp while Hilaire hopped around in anguish under a gigantic umbrella, proved the death of the telephone, and we were cut off from all communication.

Messages sent down by hand to the Postmaster producing no result for three desolate days, directly Hilaire and ' *L'homme* ' had cleared the road, I drove my skidding car down to the post-office in the town, lodged my complaint and explained our predicament.

I was met with every kind of difficulty and

objection. Everybody's line was deranged at the same moment ; our Domaine was so far away and the mechanics lost so much time getting to and from it, &c., &c. I seized upon this last excuse and offered to take a mechanic back with me then and there in my car and deliver him again to the post-office when his work was done. A doubtful silence ensued, broken by the arrival of an intelligent-looking young man in workman's overalls with a bag of tools. I had noticed him lurking in the background during my interview with the superintendent, which he had evidently overheard, and the lure of the promised joy-ride in my car had evidently proved too much for him. So I kidnapped my mechanic and the line was put right forthwith.

I have now an idea of attempting to kidnap the ancient Mayor, inviting him to *déjeuner* at the Domaine, and then driving him down the rocky and precipitous *Chemin de Malbosc* at such a terrific speed that his bones shall rattle in his skin, just to emphasise the fact that our road really does need repair.

The installation of the telephone when we first arrived was a little comedy in itself. The chief engineer waited upon me with his henchmen carrying large coils of wire, and I showed him where I wanted the apparatus to be placed in the house. Then came the question of the outside wiring and how to attach the communicating wires from the house to the main line without disfiguring the garden.

After much discussion we decided to run them down through the olive grove to a public post some metres below, but to do this the line must cross the terraces of a peasant neighbour who lived far away in the mountains. To await his permission to traverse his terraces would cause indefinite delay, and I wanted my telephone installed at once. Then suddenly the chief engineer had an inspiration. He would make a *détour* by the road and reach the telephone post below without trespassing upon the peasant's terraces. Then Hilaire should throw the coil of wire across those same terraces to him, and he would catch it and affix it to the post. In this manner not one trespassing footmark would be made upon the property of another.

And so the thing was done, amid shouts of joyous laughter.

I can see Hilaire now, bobbing up and down in his excitement and slapping his hands and thighs triumphantly as the coil of wire, well and truly thrown, whizzed through a clearing of the olive trees and was deftly caught by the engineer below—who promptly burst into victorious song.

Afterwards, of course, I celebrated the event with a glass of wine all round.

" The coil of wire ... whizzed through a clearing of the olive trees."

We cherish that hidden joke between us to this day, and whenever I meet the chief engineer, dashing about in his disreputable but so useful car, his blue eyes and strong white teeth flash with reminiscent merriment in his sun-browned face.

But the telephone is a necessary curse in Provence. Something is always going wrong with it, generally upon Sundays and Feast Days. I begin to suspect that, ninety-nine times out of a hundred, its going suddenly dumb is simply caused by the young ladies of the post-office who, when they want a little peace, just take out the plugs and disconnect the wires until a complaint is sent down to the superintendent. How otherwise account for the connection being often re-established, without a visit from a mechanic, directly the complaint has been received ?

Ah well, perhaps if I had to live with that infernal machine clamped upon my head and listen to the peremptory demands or querulous complaints of subscribers all day, I should do likewise—or worse.

In fact I think that all post-office work must be pure poison. It is intricate ; it is maddening ; and it is ill-paid. It is enough to sour the sweetest disposition, and the girls who work in post-offices are accustomed to receive nothing but complaints.

Realising from my own experience that good work is generally taken for granted whilst the smallest peccadillo is blamed, I used always to send down a huge bouquet of flowers, or an out-size box of chocolates, to encourage the staff of workers in the Hampstead Post-office who served me so well in the days when I ran a dress-designing business to help my man finish his History of the British Army.

The superintendent then informed me that it was the very first time her girls had ever received one word of thanks or encouragement—much less a gift—during the thirty years she had been in charge ; and they all subscribed to send me a long telegram of thanks which she, herself, transmitted.

I could well believe this plaint, because it was so very rare for one of my customers to ring up and ask that a message of thanks might be con-veyed to my workers for the creation of a successful gown. Those thoughtful ladies who did perform this gracious little act of courtesy were well rewarded, for ever after they had love sewn into their seams. And love is a great beautifier.

So even when I sometimes long to strangle a careless telephone operator, I also feel an under-current of sympathy for her deep down in my heart.

But there is one large, fat, relentless woman with a mouth like a spring-trap, who sits in a corner of the post-office, for whom I have no sympathy at all. Whether, under those rolls of fat, there beats a heart the size of a dried pea I have often wondered, for she shows me no mercy when Fate compels me to ask her some simple question.

At first I approached her diffidently and ingratiatingly, asking her if she would have the goodness to tell me what I wished to know. She raised her chin half an inch from its bed of fat, gave me one withering look through her *pince-nez* (why are *pince-nez* such terrifying things, almost as intimidating as a *lorgnette?*), then embedded it again, lowering her scornful eyes and silently continuing the work she was doing.

Crushing.

But I was anxious to collect an important registered packet which had arrived at the Domaine when I was out and had therefore been taken away again by the postman. He had left a message telling me that if I would go to *Guichet* No. 1 at the *Grand Bureau des Postes*, I should find my packet awaiting me. Well, I was inside the *Grand Bureau des Postes* and this implacable mass of fat was installed behind *Guichet* No. 1. I was obeying my instructions implicitly.

I tried again, this time addressing the amorphous mass politely but plaintively.

Still no result.

I was getting irritated, so once again, and in a higher and clearer tone, I repeated my inquiry, this time without the preliminary courtesies, as they appeared wasted upon her.

Then like a corpulent cobra she reared her head and spat these words at me : " *Ce n'est pas mon affaire.*" It was not her business ! Then perhaps the highest official in that post-office, the great *Receveur* (Postmaster) himself, would know whose business it was to answer polite questions with courtesy. I gently suggested this, turned on my heel, walked swiftly to the private door of the *Receveur's* office, knocked, and was admitted.

I had made the acquaintance of the *Receveur* before, when my man and I had visited him to announce our arrival and new address. He was a very beautiful person, tall, with an elegant waist, a neat pointed beard and great melting eyes, which he used on me to best advantage. When we made our farewell, he had taken my extended hand tenderly in his, as though it were a piece of precious porcelain, and bowed over it until his corsets cracked. My husband appeared to be secretly amused, and, when we were alone together in the car, remarked to me with a chuckle : " Damn it all, darling, I thought the fellow was going to kiss you." So even he had noticed that I had had a success with the *Receveur*.

The thought of that last interview strengthened my legs as I stalked across to the door of the great man. He answered my knock himself, and, when he recognised his visitor, bowed almost to the floor and swept me into his office with a marvellous all-embracing gesture.

I explained my business, and told him of the icy reception I had received from the cobra coiled up in *Guichet* No. 1. In a moment he had flung open his door opening into the post-office, and, pointing with a shaking finger towards *Guichet* No. 1, asked me if it was "*La Grasse au coin*" (the fat one in the corner) who had been unkind to me.

Then he rushed tumultuously into an inner office, extracted my little registered package, and bowed me to the main entrance. I had a vision of the whole staff of the post-office: the little wizened man who takes parcels; the young man with the smouldering dark eyes and fierce eyebrows who deals with letters and stamps; the inky youth with his hair cut *en brosse* who sends telegrams; the painted lady who takes in the savings; AND the cobra; all startled out of their usual torpor, with elongated necks, goggling eyes and loose open mouths, watching the scene.

I made a triumphal and sensational exit—WITH my parcel ; and doubtless a reproof was administered by the great *Receveur* himself to ' *La Grasse au coin.*' I hope it was.

My dignity, however, had a narrow shave the other day. I was going away for a short time, and thought that I would call for my letters at the main post-office on my way to the station, as I was to leave the Domaine before the arrival of the postman.

The boy with the smouldering eyes and fierce eyebrows informed me that unless I produced my passport or *carte d'identité* he could not give me my letters. I had neither with me, and I knew that he was within the letter of the law. In vain I pleaded that I had lived in the place for two years and had been constantly in and out of the post-office. He denied all knowledge of me, the perfidious pup, and I saw the cobra concealing a malicious smile in her corner. Of course she was delighted that someone else should thwart me— and someone with officialdom behind him.

Once more I decided to play my trump card— the *Receveur*—and in a majestic voice I demanded to see him, and assured that boy that *Monsieur le Receveur* was an old friend of mine and would immediately identify and vouch for me. The pup had perforce to go in search of the great man, and I awaited his appearance with confident patience, feeling sure that I should get my letters immediately.

Through the door of that inner office bustled a little, round, clean-shaven man with a ridiculous *béret* perched upon the side of an otherwise bald head, and little bright eyes twinkling through large horn spectacles. Across his ample tumpkin was stretched an impressive gold cable of a watch-chain—the only thing impressive about him. The sulky boy swept a gesture towards the little man and ejaculated curtly :

" *Voilà ! Monsieur le Receveur.*"

THAT—*Monsieur le Receveur ?* I was staggered. I had never set eyes upon this little round man before, nor he upon me. How could he identify a complete stranger ? Where, oh where was my handsome champion ? Was I to be humbled before that supercilious cobra and lose my dignity before them all ?

In a flash I decided to bluff. With a superb gesture of friendliness I stretched out my hand across the counter towards this strange *Receveur* and greeted him as an old friend. With my eyes I hypnotised him not to give me away. Thank heaven he responded, though for an agonising fraction of a second he paused. Then my hand was shaken, a nod was given to the sulky boy, and

I was handed my letters. The discomfited cobra coiled up again, and, with grateful thanks to *Monsieur le Receveur*, I departed swiftly.

The French really are a chivalrous people.

I saw this new *Receveur* again later. He sent me a telephone bill, on the back of which was printed, in an enclosed square to make it more conspicuous, a request that subscribers should deposit a lump sum of money for their telephone calls at the beginning of the year to save the rendering of small monthly bills. I thought this a very good idea, and so I went down to the post-office, taking with me the sum of three hundred francs to deposit.

No one there knew anything at all about this request. I inquired of one and all of the staff, and was met with blank incredulity when I informed them that a special notice desiring subscribers to deposit a lump sum was printed on the back of every telephone bill that they sent out. I referred them to the printed form itself. It was handed from hand to hand. Everyone had a look, and each in turn muttered in a voice of astonishment : " *Oui. C'est vrai !* " As if I should have troubled myself to go down there with my three hundred francs unless it had been suggested to me.

Finally the *Receveur* was fetched, and *he* had

never before remarked that notice. But he had to admit that it was there.

When I produced my bundle of franc notes everyone in the office stopped work. There was a stupefied silence, and I was the uncomfortable cynosure of all eyes.

I asked if anything was wrong with those particular notes ; or if, perhaps, I had not brought enough to deposit.

Whereupon the *Receveur* began to giggle and his sycophantic staff to do likewise.

I stood my ground, somewhat bewildered, and eventually one of them reverently picked up my notes, looked again at the funny animal who had deposited them, put them in a drawer and fumblingly wrote me a receipt.

Much mystified I took my departure, but so curious was I to know why my deposit had been received so strangely that on the way home I stopped at the house of an old English resident and described the queer scene to him.

He laughed immoderately, and when he could speak, suggested that the explanation must be that the whole staff was dumbfounded that anyone could possibly be willing to pay for something not yet had.

In France they pay only for delivered goods and consider anyone who pays in advance to be quite mad. Evidently that printed request had been issued many years ago by the post-office authorities, and, as no one had ever responded to it, they had forgotten all about it.

Last summer I had yet another unusual experience of officialdom in Provence. Emilia came up to my tower where I was describing some of my adventures in Provence for 'Maga,' and informed me that *Monsieur l'Inspecteur d'Hygiene* awaited me below. When I inquired of her his business I got, of course, his family history. He was apparently *un brave homme*, he adored his wife, who was handsome, big, and fat, and would make ten of him. They had no children, but they had a big Alsatian dog, the property of the wife, which protected their car when *Monsieur l'Inspecteur* was on his rounds. Doubtless if *Madame* peered out of the window overlooking the drive she would see the car—a *Renault*—and perhaps even the head—or tail—of the dog sticking out of the window, for the car was small and the dog was big.

Emilia skipped over to the window and craned out. No, no sign of any portion of the dog, but very certainly it was there. Again I patiently asked the man's business, and was informed that he lived three doors away from Emilia's brother-in-law, in a little flat with but three rooms but quite perfectly kept. His wife had made the lace curtains herself, and Emilia was sure that *Monsieur l'Inspecteur* had painted and distempered the walls, because he had been seen that same day with green finger-nails and a dab of paint on his nose. Evidently he had been suddenly called away on official business in the midst of his painting, and Emilia supposed that they had no turpentine in the house. They kept a very good table, because Emilia had herself seen the wife buying a fat *Bresse* chicken and a goodly quantity of vegetables in the market on Tuesday. Though to look at *Monsieur l'Inspecteur* to-day, one would never believe that he fed well, he looked sad and nervous. . . .

Here I rose to my feet and announced my intention of descending from my tower to investigate the reason for this official visit, since nothing but domestic details could be got out of Emilia.

It was a question of the canalisation of a drain that carries off the water from my kitchen sink— a tiresome affair which involved a great deal of clambering about the olive groves in the heat, and much discussion. Eventually the Inspector arrived at an agreement, and I asked him if he would like a drink before going on his way. He declined it, but suddenly paused dramatically in my rose-garden and pleaded for just one rose to put beside the portrait of his wife. Then, to my intense consternation, he began violently to weep. Through his sobs he told me that his beloved wife had died suddenly after an operation only ten days before. From his pocket he produced her photograph and a lock of her hair. He told me that she had been the best wife in the world, had always given him the choicest morsels from every dish, and that when they were cold in bed at night she would give him all the eiderdown. Such devotion ! Such care ! Such fidelity ! What a companion ! His voice was lost in sobs.

I patted his poor shaking shoulder ; I picked him the loveliest roses in my garden ; I gave him a basket of peaches ; I spent a whole hour trying to console him a little. I had actually got him dry and quiet when at last we reached his waiting car. But all my hard work was undermined immediately when a large Alsatian dog, curled up on the back seat of the car, sat up and pawed a welcome to his master.

Her dog !—and the sobs broke out afresh.

The poor little man drove off embowered in roses, tears streaming down his face, with the great Alsatian dog, reared up on its hind-legs, towering behind him, its paws on his shoulders, as though ready to direct his confused driving.

Her dog. . . .

I walked slowly back to the house. There was no time to dress for dinner—I was very late as it was—so I walked straight into *Monsieur's* great *Galerie* where he was awaiting me with impatience.

"AT LAST," he ejaculated irritably. "Why *will* these tiresome people always come to see you just before meals? Well, what did that interminable little talker come about?"

"Drains," I replied in a muffled voice.

I was standing over my man's chair, and suddenly he screwed in his eye-glass and looked sharply at me.

"What is it, sweetheart?" he asked gently.

And then I poured forth an incoherent story of drains, handsome wives, locks of hair, eiderdowns, choice morsels, cars, roses, tears, operations, Alsatian dogs—and death. The pathetic jumble that, after all, makes up life.

Somehow he understood. He always did.

DRIVING A CAR.

WHEN we finally decided to dig up our roots from English soil and go out to live in Provence to bask henceforth in the sun, I was much exercised in mind as to whether or no I would take with me my faithful little Morris-Oxford coupé car, ' Sir William.' He had always been such a gallant, loyal little chap, never once letting me down during all the mad adventures we had shared together, never complaining or going on strike even when I took him up into the wilds of Scotland and left him for three weeks parked under a tree in the rain while I camped in a tent on the mountain above. In those days he was plain ' William '; but such was his courage, chivalry, and resolution, that, when his inventor was knighted, I knighted ' William ' also. I hope his present owner has now elevated him to the peerage, because, in the end, it was decided that ' William ' and I must part.

This decision gave me a real pang, but experts whom I consulted at the A.A. advised me to buy a Fiat car for three reasons : first, because the

Fiat engines are powerful enough to climb the side of a house, and I should be perpetually climbing mountains; secondly, because a Fiat has marvellous brakes and is practically guaranteed not to skid; and thirdly, because, like a taxi, it turns in its own length, and so avoids the agony of manœuvring at hairpin bends.

As I had never driven in a mountainous country (one can hardly call the mountains of Perthshire real mountains), my A.A. expert deemed it safer for me, and for possible passengers, to sell 'William' and buy a Fiat.

The enormous tax upon an English car, and also the fact that ' William's ' driving-wheel was on the right side instead of the left, finally settled the question; and, with a sad farewell pat on his faithful nose, I left ' Sir William ' in the care of a kind Morris agent with a plea that he would find an appreciative master for him. I hope he did.

The testing and choosing of the new Fiat was a hair-raising business. I told the youthful agent that I wanted a car that would not easily skid and with powerful brakes. A dangerous twinkle came into his eyes as he invited me to enter the latest model for a demonstration of its powers. I entered it and he took the wheel. We climbed a steep and tortuous mountain road with extraordinary ease and speed. Then he turned the car and began to descend. The road was of asphalt. It began to rain. The surface was as slippery as glass. That young devil at the wheel accelerated violently, and we tore down the mountain at breakneck speed. At every corner he suddenly put on the brakes. I was petrified—he seemed to be deliberately trying to make the car skid. He was, as I afterwards learned.

We entered the town at the same headlong speed, and it seemed to me that nothing on earth could save the life of the policeman on point duty directly in front of us. Suddenly we stopped absolutely dead within a foot of him; I shot forward and nearly broke my nose on the windscreen, and the policeman roared with laughter, tapped his own nose, and doubled up again.

A splendid joke !

I looked reproachfully at my driver. I wondered if I had aged perceptibly during that mad career down the mountain and through the town. He was regarding me with dancing, triumphant eyes.

" Well, Madame," he said in French, " are you now satisfied that the brakes of a Fiat car are good and that she does not easily skid, or shall I give you another demonstration ? "

Heaven forbid ! I told him that I was more than satisfied, and then complimented him ironically upon his wonderful driving. He informed me that his great hobby was car-racing in the Italian mountains, so that he had had some useful experience. I ordered my car ; delivery was promised for a month hence, and I returned, shattered, to my hotel.

I will not describe the full perfidy of that young descendant of Ananias, or the lies he told us to explain the non-arrival of our car upon the promised date. Suffice it to say that Fiat headquarters had removed their agency from him the day before I called for my demonstration, and, unable to resist the temptation of securing one last order and commission, he had omitted to tell me that in selling me that Fiat he was performing an illegal act. We were embroiled in the row that followed, and the car had finally to be extracted by a lawyer, and eventually arrived three months late.

Before her arrival my Fiat was christened ' Desirée ' by our builder's chauffeur-son, because she was *Desirée mais pas trouvée*, as the French write on their memorial stones—desired, nay, longed for, but found not.

It was maddening and very expensive, that period of waiting ; for we had to get from our hired flat to our Domaine daily to superintend the enlargement of the little Provençal cottage that we had bought some distance away. Sometimes we walked; at other times, when we had packages to take across, we hired a car; and very often Léon, the builder's son, gave us lifts in his little lorry—nicknamed 'Consuelo' (Consolation) by me—and we bumped down mountain tracks in company with sacks of cement, scaffolding-poles, workmen's tools: and very frequently there was a goodly company of the workmen themselves, heavily perfumed from the popular Provençal breakfast of slices of garlic, layers of anchovies, and cheese laid between thick slices of bread. 'Consuelo' was a good-hearted wench, and never seemed to resent her over-laden state.

In fact, cars in Provence are nearly always as kindly and accommodating as their Provençal owners, and even English cars soon learn the habit of hospitality. I am thinking chiefly of 'Gracie,' the unlovely car of a lovely person. 'Gracie,' like 'Desirée,' was promised for a certain date, but failed to appear. Her purchaser being a young Englishwoman of spirit who, having lived all her life in Provence, long ago realised that strong measures must be taken to get things done, sent a mechanic all the way to the Paris factory to inspect and bring home her new car. When he reached there he found that the car had not yet been painted, but his instructions were to

bring back that car whatever its condition, so long
as the engine was good. Therefore he drove
'Gracie' back in triumph. She has never been
painted to this day. She has never had time to
be painted, her life has been too full and too
philanthropic. She has effected household re-
movals; she has carried the sick to hospital;
she does all the household marketing for her
mistress, and frequently for her mistress's neighbours; she climbs incredibly steep and rocky
mountains carrying sometimes as many as sixteen
laughing adults and children (not to mention
an enormous bull-terrier) to enjoy hilarious picnics,
returning home at night with her load increased
perhaps by mountain boulders to form a new
rock-garden, baskets of fruit presented by peasant
friends, and decorated within and without with
branches of trees and bouquets of mountain
flowers to adorn the hospitable, elastic-sided villa
of her owner.

That owner, when teased about her 'Gracie's'
very ungraceful appearance, merely tosses her
small head, and, shaking the hair out of twinkling
blue eyes, defies criticism and resolutely refuses
to 'make up' 'Gracie's' face in the prevailing
fashion. There is not, never has been, and never
shall be any nonsense about 'Gracie.' And think
of the joy and liberty of possessing a car that has

no enamel to be spoiled either by rain or by careless drivers !

When our ' Desirée ' did at last arrive, she
really was a dainty little baggage.   She was
enamelled a beautiful shade of *grenat* (garnet),
and her upholstery and carpet matched the
enamel.   She glittered with chromium.   Personally
I prefer male cars—less capricious and tempera-
mental, and I still mourned my reliable little
' Sir William.'   But ' Desirée ' was already named
for me, and I had to accept her femininity with a
good grace.

She has proved to be rather a minx, but, like
the majority of minxes, intelligent and attractive.
Her greatest fault (shared, perhaps, by her mistress) is a marked reluctance to be roused in the
morning.   Once started (also like her mistress),
she becomes charged with a superabundance of
energy, and is ready and willing to tackle any
obstacle and climb over it.

But I regret to say that she is a snob.   It may
be that she has caught the infection from the
Riviera coast, for she adores racing down to
Cannes and prinking along the Croisette, the
admired of all.   In vain I tell her that she must
learn to live the life of the peasants in the mountains, as we do ; but I fear that in her heart she
looks down upon us for rising early, lunching at

noon, dining at seven o'clock, and going to bed early. I feel sure that she would prefer to rest in her garage all the morning and be parked at night among the Hispano-Suizas and other *voitures-de-luxe* outside a coast casino till the small hours of the morning.

Certain it is that when I try to rout her out to come to the market with me to collect Emilia and her baskets, 'Desirée' is often very sulky and tiresome. I am sure she considers such a journey beneath her dignity. She spits and swears and refuses to start, until I am obliged to fetch Hilaire to coax her to move. Any man is better than none, it appears, since she does for him what she utterly refuses to do for me, and then rushes off with a great display of her prowess and power—showing off before Hilaire, of course. To cure her conceit I make her pick up every peasant we meet laden with a basket or dripping with rain.

Monsieur, always susceptible to beauty, grace, and vivacity in things feminine, was entirely captivated by 'Desirée' from the beginning. He was even apt to forget our faithful little 'Sir William' until Madame, inflamed by what he called her "raging sense of equity," reminded him of their willing little slave. Then he would say : " Yes, ' William ' was a good little chap.

He served us well," to comfort me, and then spoil the effect of this generous tribute by adding, " But I *do* love our ' Desirée.' "

When she first arrived it was necessary that I should have a few lessons in her management, she was so entirely different from ' Sir William ' in make and build. So we engaged a Provençal chauffeur, one Pascal, who also possesses a Fiat lady, to give me instruction.

Monsieur, of course, insisted upon accompanying us on this preliminary venture. Such was his unbounded faith in his wife that he was quite willing to risk his precious life with her, and no pleas that his presence would make her all the more nervous would deter him.

We all started off together up a steep mountain road, where my instructor made me stop and start again, and repeat this trying and perfectly maddening performance until I could do it without allowing ' Desirée ' to run backwards. Then he suggested a little drive to a certain historic castle.

Being strangers in the province, Monsieur and I had not the faintest idea where we were going—but we were soon to find out.

My instructor directed me to a narrow road winding up a mountain, and I faithfully obeyed his orders. At first the ground was almost level on either side, and I drove happily on. Gradually the ascent became more steep, and the drop on the right side of the road, where I was, of course, driving, still steeper. Soon I found myself hugging the edge of a positive precipice with no protecting parapet. With eyes on stalks I drove on, wondering what would happen if we met another car descending. Dreadful bends in the road lay ahead ; it became narrower and narrower, and more and more steep, as it wound its way upward under a huge frowning cliff of rock. Only here and there was there just room for a car to pass. I became very silent and hoped that my instructor could not hear the beating of my heart, which sounded to me deafening. Monsieur, in the back seat, had also become very silent, and I hoped that he was wrapped in ecstatic contemplation of the ravine and distant view, which I knew must be marvellous, though I dared not move my eyes from the road. He confided to me afterwards that he also was wondering what on earth would happen if we suddenly met a *char-à-banc*.

And we suddenly did !

It roared round a corner with no warning whatsoever. There was no room to pass. Its driver jammed on his brakes with a screaming sound ; I applied mine, and ' Desirée,' mercifully, stopped dead. I sat quite still and informed Pascal that he could now take the wheel, and that

Monsieur and I would descend while he backed the car along the edge of that precipice until he found a place wide enough for two cars to pass.

We then got out, and I clung to a pine-tree overhanging the ravine, while Pascal, with a very tight mouth, backed the car gingerly some hundreds of metres, Monsieur following him and shouting warnings when the wheels went too near that awful edge.

The people in the *char-à-banc* laughed heartily as they passed me clinging to my pine, but the chauffeur leaned out and heartily damned my eyes in a torrent of angry French.

Once again seated in ' Desirée,' I generously allowed my instructor to keep the wheel for the remainder of the ascent. I asked him why the chauffeur of the *char-à-banc* had so abused me, and he laughed and told me that it was because we were doing a forbidden thing. Apparently this was a one-way road ; the ascent thereof had long since been forbidden because of constant landslides on the side of the ravine—the side upon which we were driving at that moment. The chauffeur of the *char-à-banc* had not sounded his horn when rounding that corner because he naturally did not expect to meet an ascending car.

When I indignantly inquired of Pascal why he had brought us up that way, he laughed and said that he had done it on purpose, thinking that if Madame first drove along so dangerous a road she would never again be nervous of any other.

It was the toss of a half-penny that he did not destroy my nerve for ever, but luckily his experiment proved successful, and I have never since been intimidated by another road after that first terrifying experience.

We had not the heart to scold the intrepid Pascal, because he is such a charming person. He has helped us in a thousand ways since we came out to Provence, and has a happy knack of always arriving upon the scene at a crisis and helping us out of it. Monsieur was always convinced that the man has Devon blood ; for he is never so happy as when doing someone else's job, and talks incessantly while performing it.

His one great failing is that he WILL NOT send in his bills punctually, so that, when they arrive, their proportions are alarming. Over and over again had I warned him that if he did not change his methods I should be obliged to change my garagist. But he never mended his ways, and gradually I began to employ other mechanics when ' Desirée ' was out of sorts. Yet, by some fatality, invariably when some crisis occurs, Pascal is the only man available to deal with it. I ring up every other garage in the town before seeking his aid, but always their owners are out on some expedition or otherwise prevented from coming, and, in the end, comes the inevitable Pascal, beaming and triumphant, every line on his expressive face seeming to say, " There you are, you see ! You can't get on without Pascal ! "

Presumptuously I thought that I could begin to teach a little friend of mine to drive ' Desirée.' I imagined that if I drove the car out of the garage on to the drive, we could sit side by side in it, and I could instruct my novice in the mysteries of gears and gear-changing while the car was stationary.

Accordingly I began my lesson and all went very well, though both instructress and pupil found it a trifle dull just going through the motions of gear-changing and not moving an inch.   Then it occurred to me that I would teach her the use of clutch and accelerator, and that no harm could possibly come to us if I started the engine and we just crawled gently down the drive.   I had driven for so many years myself that I had forgotten the blind panic that sometimes descends upon a beginner and causes him or her to stamp violently upon the accelerator, and then lose his or her head.

This was exactly what happened.   ' Desirée ' sprang forward like a startled kangaroo ; her driver's one thought was to find the foot-brake and then stamp upon it, and she entirely forgot that it was also necessary to steer. In an instant we had careered madly over the edge of the drive into a bed of roses and anemones on a lower level, and were making straight for a huge Provençal oil jar full of trailing geraniums. It seemed quite certain that 'Desirée' must charge it and break her pretty nose. The one thought that flashed comfort into my brain at that awful moment was that Hilaire had gone home for his luncheon and was not witnessing the destruction of his flower-bed and grass border. His howls of anguish would have totally unnerved me.

Fortunately in one way and unfortunately in another, the ground was soft from recent rain, and the two wheels on the left side sank deep and ever deeper into the soil and so checked our headlong career. The car stopped dead, firmly fixed in the flower-bed at an angle of forty-five.

I then took the wheel and tried to back her out, but, of course, could not move her. The engine roared, but nothing happened. Hopeless. The only thing to do was to ring up a garage and get professional help. But I had forgotten that the hour of noon had struck and that all good Provençaux would have left their work until 2 P.M. The knowledge that Hilaire would be back before long and would see this humiliating sight forced me to attempt the apparently impossible.

Desperately I telephoned everywhere, but only the last garage replied. The cheerful voice of Pascal answered me, and when he heard of our predicament, he chuckled and assured me that he would be at the Domaine in ten minutes.

He arrived. He worked like seven men. He gradually levered up 'Desirée' with the aid of my crick and his own, while my unfortunate little friend and I, Emilia, and Lucienne hung on to the car on the farther side. Planks were inserted under the wheel, and very gradually 'Desirée' was hoisted out of the mud and driven safely on to the drive.

I have never seen a man so hot as was Pascal. He poured and he mopped and he poured again. He was blinded with the sweat of his brow, and little rivulets streamed down his nose and fell in a shower from his moustache. He melted visibly before our eyes. (These details may sound disgusting, but I had never watched a man actually dissolving before.) Yet when the disinterment of 'Desirée' was accomplished, Pascal was still in his element, energetic, and untiring, bossing us all in a magnificent manner.

We were one and all despatched to fetch gardening tools, to repair, as far as possible, the damage done to the flower-bed before Hilaire should return. Emilia, her black eyes sparkling with excitement and fun, the skirt of her mauve overall pulled over her head to protect it from the fierce noonday sunshine, was soon down on all fours levering the crushed turf of the border to ground level with a small gardening fork, while her bland-ishing tongue poured flatteries over Pascal for his wonderful work. Lucienne scrattled among the anemones with a trowel to regain a smooth appear-ance ; I applied splints to the fractured bough of a rose-bush ; my little friend raked the gravel of the drive, while Pascal replaced the borrowed planks in the wood-shed below and put back the tools into our respective cars. He had hardly garaged ' Desirée,' washed his hands in the kitchen sink, drunk a reviving glass of wine, and departed amid a fluster of congratulations and thanks, when Hilaire appeared at the top of the garden and descended the terrace steps, looking sus-piciously around him, obviously scenting trouble of some sort with the curious animal instinct I have often remarked in him.

We all shot indoors before he observed us, like a pack of guilty children, and, when he passed the Galerie window—and, of course, peered in—we were all seated at the table innocently eating our belated luncheon, with a flushed Lucienne waiting on us.

Even so, Hilaire appeared uneasy. He paused,
sniffed the air more suspiciously and looked about

" Down on all fours levering the crushed turf."

him. Then he began to make a tour of the garden
—in search of he knew not what. But fortunately
he did not look to his left as he walked down the

185

drive to the front gates, or else he must inevitably have seen the newly turned earth of the flower-bed and the slight grooves still apparent in his grass border. It was not until three days later that he appeared at the kitchen door holding the little gardening fork with which Emilia had endeavoured to lever up the turf. She had carefully replaced that fork where she had found it, but had omitted to clean it first. Now Hilaire invariably cleans and polishes all his tools after use, and, therefore, finding this muddy little fork in a corner, knew at once that someone had been meddling with his tools. The question again arose in his mind, what had we been up to during his absence three days ago?

He held up the little fork accusingly before Emilia's eyes and shook it at her; but, born actress as she is, she merely gazed blankly at it and asked Hilaire if he had gone a little mad, shrugged her shoulders, and went on scraping carrots, perched on a wall in the sunshine, her little fat legs dangling.

When Hilaire had trudged away, discomfited, those small fat feet of Emilia's, in their shabby slippers, beat a silent but triumphant tattoo upon the wall, and she shied a carrot at the giggling Lucienne who had watched the little scene delightedly from an upper window. (So had I.)

But Hilaire's sixth sense was aroused, and, in spite of Emilia's acting, he made another exhaustive search of the garden, and at last found the incriminating dents in his precious grass. But all his questioning and accusations never got the truth out of Emilia, who lied shamelessly and supposed that those marks had been made by some careless visiting car when we were all from home.

After this experience, I thought it wiser that my little friend should take lessons from a professional, one Paul, who had taught both the famous Maurice Chevalier and Mdlle. Mistinguet to drive in Paris, when he was electrician at the *Casino de Paris*.

It is always worth while to listen to the past histories of the people one meets out here, and one gets delicious surprises. For instance, the smart, boyish, little chauffeuse of a neighbour of mine was one of France's most expert parachutists, but, as everyone must live and one cannot descend from the skies in a parachute every day, she had decided to take up more regular work.

Nearly all the chauffeurs of Provence are *hommes-à-tout-faire* (men of all work) and combine a variety of jobs ; but the most versatile of my acquaintance is Jean, the servant of a celebrated little Comtesse. Primarily he is her *chef*, attired in spotless white, and there is nothing that he cannot cook, from rare savoury dishes to luscious cakes and fairy pastry. Occasionally a deft butler waits at table wearing black trousers, white

" Primarily he is her chef . . . Occasionally a deft butler . . . It is Jean."

coat, and black tie. It is Jean. Perhaps Madame la Comtesse kindly proposes to send a guest home in her car, and in a few minutes a smart liveried chauffeur drives up to the door—Jean again.

188

Strolling round her beautiful garden, friends will come upon a gay young man clad only in blue workman's trousers and a sleeveless vest, splashing fresh paint upon a rose trellis, carolling strains from opera the while. They make some pleasant remark ; the man turns round and they recognise Jean. In the early morning he will be seen running madly down the mountains followed by three wire-haired terriers, exercising the dogs before breakfast, for they are his especial care. These are only a few of the activities of Jean, and he is typical of many servants here. In Provence one never hears that dreadful sniffy remark : " That is not my work " ; rather, the workers welcome any occupation other than their own—or beside their own.

They would delight my mother could she see and hear them. I shall never forget her face as she told the story of an English countrywoman seeing off her young daughter at the station. The girl was going to her first place as scullery-maid in a great house. Her mother kissed her good-bye, and, pushing her into a third class carriage, thus admonished her from the platform : " Now remember ! Eat as *much* as yer can. Do as *little* as yer can. And ef yer don't like it—*come 'ome !* "

My mother, who throughout her life never lost a maid except through marriage, came home to us and remarked that it was small wonder that the old spirit of loyalty and loving service was dying out in England if the mothers of prospective domestic servants instilled such principles into their young.

The Provençal children are taught early to do every kind of work, and one is continually surprised to find skill, dexterity, and resource in unexpected places, and blesses it.

One terribly wet day in winter I was obliged to go out in the car on some errand which took me along a curly, asphalted mountain road. It was raining so hard that even my electric windscreen wiper, working feverishly, could not help my vision, and I did not see, in time, a fall of soil which had slid down the mountain on to the road. When I saw it I swerved, but, being startled, did not immediately twist back the steering-wheel. Easily guided by a finger-touch, in a moment 'Desirée' had shot over the edge of the road into a shallow gully—at least, the two left wheels were in the gully and the other two still on the road, a repetition of the experience at the Domaine which I have already described, only here there was no hope of a rescuing Pascal.

I managed to clamber out of the opposite door, and stood in cataracts of rain gazing at my ditched 'Desirée' and feeling an awful fool.

But I have long since proved that a special Providence watches over fools, if they are well-intentioned fools, and I felt certain that someone or other would come along sometime or other and rescue this fool somehow or other. The moment of rescue did not, however, appear imminent. The afternoon light was fading; I was twenty kilometres from home, and at least sixteen from the nearest town and telephone, on a deserted mountain road in such streaming rain that it seemed very unlikely that any Provençal would be out in it.

I cowered under a hedge, lit a cigarette, and thanked heaven there had not been a ravine on the left side of the road, as there usually is on our mountain tracks. I resigned myself to a long wait, and my only fear was that Monsieur would grow anxious about me. Then I remembered that he always laughingly told our friends that when once his wife went out in the car he never expected her back until she appeared; for she always thought of a thousand and one urgent things that must be done, and had far too many peasant friends who confided to her all their family histories. Perhaps he would have his tea without me.

Suddenly I heard a muffled roar in the distance. It must be a lorry coming round the bend. I jumped up and went and stood in the middle of the road as I saw a *camion* approaching, and then I clasped my hands together in an attitude of prayer and shook them above my head at the driver. There were three men huddled together on the driver's seat, and, to my relief, directly they saw my draggled figure, there was a grinding of brakes, and the lorry slid to a standstill. I pointed to my poor ditched ' Desirée ' and beat upon my breast, whereupon three sets of white teeth flashed simultaneously, and three pairs of legs dangled over the edge of the *camion* and then jumped to the ground.

Not much explanation was needed; my predicament spoke for itself, and those three men set to work at once—and HOW they worked! The driver, a slim boy in thin cotton workman's overalls, crawled under the car and lay on his tumpkin in the mud, while the other two men swiftly destroyed a perfectly good wall on the other side of the road and brought huge boulders across to him. These he banked one upon the other in true Provençal wall-building fashion in the gully under the suspended wheels. Then the other two cricked up the car a little higher with a mighty crick from the *camion's* tool-box, and rolled more boulders under the car to be placed in like manner.

Of course, as the gully gradually became filled up with stones, the torrents of rain flowing off the road and down the mountain into it became dammed up, so that the driver of the lorry, lying in the gully under my car, was soon immersed in water. But still he laboured on, shouting his instructions to his comrades and joking encouragement to me, until by slow degrees a causeway had been built up under the car. He then emerged, muddy and dripping, and drove 'Desirée' triumphantly back on to the road. During this laborious performance, all the men had vainly tried to persuade me to take shelter in their lorry while they did the work. Madame must take cover—Madame would get wet. Madame naturally preferred to share the soaking of her gallant rescuers, and spent her time trying to hold empty sacks over their labouring shoulders as they worked, to protect them in some measure from the pitiless downpour, since she was not allowed to carry heavy boulders for them.

When that wonderful piece of wall building was accomplished, the little driver insisted upon taking my car for a trial trip down the mountain before I entered it again, to make sure that the steering was undamaged and that I should come to no harm on my homeward drive. Of course, I insisted upon accompanying him, though I had to

193

wrangle with him for some time in the rain before this was permitted.

Fortunately no vital harm had been done. When I attempted to thank my three deliverers, and emptied out the contents of my purse to be shared amongst them, they flatly refused to take even a *franc*. They said they were very sure that, had they been in like trouble and Madame had found them, she would have done all in her power to help them ; that accidents happened to us all—and so on.

Only by great persistence, and by pointing out to them that their timely help had saved me very great expense—for it would have been necessary for me to get a garagist to come out from a distant town—could I persuade them to accept what I offered—a very inadequate reward in any case.

Then we all shook hands warmly, and I expressed a hope that when I met my three friends again it would be under happier and drier conditions.

As I drove off they were all busily engaged in destroying their causeway and rebuilding the wall they had taken down on the other side of the road.

Before leaving them I had ascertained the address of their employer—a seed and forage merchant—and I took Monsieur to visit them all and to thank them, with his beautiful courtesy, for their great kindness to his wife. Needless to say, they were all engaged in complicated work quite other than that of wall building and car driving.

A minor accident of quite another sort happened to me the other day when driving down to the coast. A beautiful great dog bounded without warning across the road directly in front of my car. All my insides changed places as I swerved instinctively and just missed him. But my right wing caught a stone pillar of a gate. Only a damaged mudguard, but it spoiled ' Desirée's ' beauty ; and, while I was examining the damage and apologising to her, a voluble townsman came up from a distance and lectured me in torrents of clipped French. Apparently he himself had passed that same stone pillar not three minutes before I scraped it. His life would have been endangered —perhaps ended—had he been there still. He would certainly have been crushed instead of the mudguard. Madame was silly and sentimental like all Englishwomen ; she would risk lives of harmless pedestrians to save that of a stupid dog. In future Madame must crush dogs, crush them always, crush them relentlessly if they got in her way. " *Il faut les écraser, Madame,*" he shouted, and then repeated over and over again that he had only just passed that spot, and had he walked there three minutes later he would doubtless have been killed and Madame would have been a murderess.

A peasant who had joined the group doffed his *béret* and hoped that Madame was unhurt, adding reassuringly that *le beau chien*, whose life Madame had saved by her presence of mind, was now safely with his owner.

As I drove away, that little townsman was still excitedly explaining the narrow escape he had had to a bored clump of people who all looked as if they wished that he *had* passed the fatal spot three minutes later.

We have had many adventures on that particular road, and there is one corner of it that I can never pass without a reminiscent chuckle. Monsieur and I had been invited to a luncheon party at an important villa on the coast. Needless to say, our departure had been retarded, as always, by an agitated Hilaire, who, although we had tiptoed secretly out to the garage to avoid his inevitable onslaught, had heard me starting up the engine. He rushed straight in front of the car as I was driving it out, having learned from past experience the only way to stop Madame when she is trying to escape him, and stood there pouring forth lists of urgent needs for the garden and the animals. He wanted birch brooms to sweep up the fallen fig-leaves that were rotting

his blessed *gazon* (grass) ; the supply of bran
had run out, and how could he feed sixteen young
rabbits if Madame did not bring him back a sack
of bran ? There was very little green stuff to be
found on the mountains in the hot weather,
&c., &c. And was it the pleasure of Madame to
have more young salads ? If so, would she please
bring him back some lettuce seed. Might he
order some more manure from his cousin ? Manure
was, he knew, expensive, but without it vegetables
would not grow ; the rabbits justified their ex-
istence by providing a certain amount of it, and
he used this very sparingly, but—and so forth
and so on.

Monsieur, driven nearly frantic by the impeding
Hilaire hopping about between the front wheels
of the car, laid his hand, as though by accident,
upon the electric siren attached to the driving-
wheel, and the ear-splitting screech that rent the
air so petrified Hilaire that he stood rigid, his
gesticulating arms stiff with shock. Then, catching
the twinkle behind Monsieur's eye-glass, he broke
into a toothless grin, took the delicate hint and
jumped aside.

With a wave of the hand and a little reassuring
word thrown out of the window as I passed him,
we drove past Hilaire with a swirl. Two kilometres from home I realised that he had forgotten

to fill up my petrol tank, which was now dangerously low. I hardly dared to break this news to
Monsieur, for we were late already, and to stop
and fill up the tank would mean yet more delay ;
but I realised that if we got stuck far from human
habitation we might never get to that luncheon
at all.

I had, however, once more forgotten the hour.
It was half-past twelve and all garages and petrol
stations would already be shut for *déjeuner*. We
passed several in the town, but not one showed a
sign of life. We must just go on and hope to
find a petrol pump whose owner was neither eating
nor sleeping.

Luck favoured us, and at a certain corner I
spied a pump standing outside a little wooden
shanty whose door was still open. I drew up and
blew my horn. Out came a fat Frenchman, who,
when I asked him to fill up my tank, looked
resentfully at his watch and informed me in a
grumbling tone that everyone to-day seemed to
want petrol and that he had already waited half
an hour for his *déjeuner*. I smiled upon him and
told him that we were just as hungry as he was,
and that if he did not give me petrol Monsieur
and I could never get to our *déjeuner* and should
be obliged to ask him to share his with us.

This frightful threat decided him to do as I

asked. He filled the tank ; I paid him for the petrol, and gave him a good tip for obliging us. He bowed to us, entered his wooden hut, and then slammed the door and locked it noisily behind him.

Monsieur, with a tremendous sigh of pent-up irritation and relief, relaxed in his seat and exhaled a cloud of cigarette smoke as I drove off with a rush.

After a while I heard a queer swishing sound, and remarked upon it. " Only a dead branch caught under the mudguard," Monsieur reassured me as I slackened pace. " Oh, GO ON, darling ! " And I went on.

Well, that puzzling noise did not sound serious, and I simply dared not stop the car again to get out and inspect. So we drove rapidly on, and at length arrived at the great gates of the villa. All the way up that long and winding drive, with its beautifully smooth surface of raked grey granite chips, I still heard that mysterious sound, but I had grown used to it, and it no longer troubled me.

On the steps of the villa stood a young man in silent convulsions of laughter. He was unknown to us both, and I thought this a very strange greeting to two perfect strangers. He tried to speak, choked, and tried again. Then he pointed at ' Desirée.' Monsieur and I turned round, and then we realised the cause of this man's unseemly mirth. For 'Desirée' had a long, long tail. The owner of the petrol pump, in his hurry and anxiety to get to his vegetable soup, had forgotten to detach the hose-pipe from our tank. The pipe was evidently rotten, my brisk departure had severed it from the pump, and we had dragged it with us for twelve kilometres. Had the hose-pipe not been rotten, I suppose we might have carried off the pump as well.

" ' Desirée ' gracefully wagging her tail the whole way."

The young man, standing upon the steps of the villa, had watched our triumphant approach up that long drive, with 'Desirée' gracefully wagging her tail the whole way. The beautiful gravel drive was scored by a sinuous line from the great gates to the front door.

The description of our arrival at the villa was recounted with enormous success at luncheon. But when the time came for our return journey,

the problem was to find a lid for our petrol tank ;
for, if I had unwittingly stolen his hose-pipe, the
owner of the pump still retained my lid.

A crowd of laughing chauffeurs from all the
guests' cars surrounded my poor humiliated ' Desirée,' each trying to devise some temporary cover
for the aperture in the tank. But it was the cook
of the villa (why had not we consulted her at
first ?) who eventually produced a small earthen-
ware cooking utensil which she placed, inverted,
over the hole, binding it on with greased paper
and string in the way one covers a pot of jam.

And so, at last, we got home.

A queer, fascinating life we live in this Paradise,
Provence. It might very well be described in
Gilbert's phrase, " a bundle of contradictions, a
mass of incongruities." Two instances will suffice
to describe it.

Having worked with our respectively serious
and frivolous pens all the morning, Monsieur and
I were spending an afternoon helping Hilaire
prepare our surplus vegetables for sale, washing
them in the great irrigation tank on the top terrace,
matching them, cutting their stalks to the same
length, and then tying them into bundles of ten
or a dozen in the neat French way. Monsieur
clad in blue workman's overalls, a loose silk handkerchief knotted fichu-fashion round his neck

instead of a collar, and a great Provençal straw hat sheltering his historian's head lest the dates therein should get dried up. Madame attired likewise, and revelling in the freedom of trousers and bare feet—when suddenly Emilia appeared, bouncing from step to step up the stone stairways like a little indiarubber ball.

Panting, she arrived at the top, announcing aloud the very thought of Madame: "*Pouff! Je deviens de plus en plus boule!*" Then when we had all laughed a little at Emilia's increasing rotundity, she whispered excitedly: "*Madame! Du monde qui arrive!*"

Visitors coming up the drive. Heavens—and it was true! Peering from our height, we saw a luxurious car approaching the house, and went down at once to receive some 'People of Importance' just as we were. And our visitors evinced no surprise at our unconventional attire, but seemed rather to envy it.

On another evening, Hilaire, Monsieur, and I, grubby and dishevelled, were busily chasing rabbits, trying to separate different breeds, when interrupted by the sudden shrilling of the telephone bell within the house. I answered it, to find that we were invited to a gala dinner at a great house on the coast to meet distinguished officers of the Mediterranean Fleet. Just time for a hurried tub and a quick change into evening clothes, and we were racing down towards Cannes in 'Desirée.' A curious mixture of smart, social, and pure peasant life.

But although occasional 'jollies' of the typical Riviera type are delightful *pour changer les idées*, Monsieur always remarked upon the headlong speed with which Madame drove home afterwards.

" 'Desirée's ' nose is towards her stable," he would say with a contented smile.

And as we drew into the mountain track leading to our little Domaine, always at a given spot just within sight of its honey-coloured walls, 'Desirée' would be made to pause while together we looked at the lovely familiar view. The plains of olive groves far below, broken by many a rounded hill; the sun glinting upon the windows of the little Provençal farmsteads; dark cypresses stabbing the skyline, and far away the blue encircling sea and the satisfying flanking line of the Estorel mountains.

Then the procedure was always the same, and our great contentment found the same expression.

One evening, lovelier than the rest—a loveliness that positively hurt—I was driving home alone in 'Desirée.' As I rounded the last bend of our lane, I saw that our favourite spot was already occupied—by another Fiat car.

It was a little two-seater, and its occupants, a boy and a girl, sat bathed in a roseate glory of sunset light. But they were not watching the mountains being transformed into a chain of amethysts and the sea into one great opal; nor did they seem to appreciate the showers of roses and geraniums dripping over the walls of the Domaine, each blossom seeming to have been dipped in fire. Perhaps it was the effect of the new moon, rising like a silver sickle above the mountains, or it may have been the air, heavy with the scent of flowers, that had gone to their heads. Anyhow, they were locked in so ecstatic an embrace that they remained quite unaware of my approach.

Their absorption in each other reminded me of another boy and girl, seated upon the deserted shore at Nice, silhouetted against the flaming splendour of sunset sky and luminous sea. The whole population of the town seemed to have congregated upon the Promenade des Anglais to watch that glorious sunset. But in the foreground sat the little couple locked in each other's arms and quite unaware of either the sunset before them or the watching crowd behind them. Rather lovely, I thought. So now I felt embarrassed. Somehow it seemed sacrilege to rend that quiet evening air and to shatter that pretty idyll by sounding a motor siren, yet I knew that Monsieur would be awaiting my return with impatience and that Emilia's *soufflé* would be spoiled if I did not.

Then Hilaire solved my problem for me. Quite evidently he had been spying upon the unconscious couple. He is incurably romantic and is the bane of all lovers who, from time to time, lurk in the lane bordering our garden, for he stalks them noiselessly and contrives to find work where, hidden by vines, he can see without being seen. Suddenly some unconquerable sneeze will betray his presence, or seeing Monsieur or Madame coming out of the house to work with him, he cannot resist a welcoming shout, and *les amoureux* will make a hurried and indignant departure.

Now, seeing my car, he let forth his usual yell, " *Voilà, Madame !* " loud enough to apprise Monsieur and Emilia, within the house, of my impending arrival.

Poetry was at once translated into prose. A flustered youth cast one startled glance in front and then behind him, and, seeing my waiting car, hurriedly started up his engine while the maiden swiftly combed her curls, and the little Fiat car fled up the lane.

As I drove through the gates of the Domaine and up the drive, Hilaire, grinning all over his face, thundered after me to open the garage.

" Madame ! " he shouted excitedly, " *C'était un Fiat !* " Madame told him that she had already remarked that the obstructing car was a Fiat.

" Fiat ! *Voiture dangereuse !* " he remarked,

" *Faites Ici Amour Toujours.*"

tapping his old nose. " Why should a Fiat car be specially dangerous ? " I inquired.

" *Fiat. F-I-A-T,*" spelled Hilaire triumphantly to a mystified Madame. " *F*aites *I*ci *A*mour *T*oujours," then slapped his knees and doubled up with silent laughter.

FEAST DAYS.

WE ran out of butter to-day. Emilia, my little *bonne*, confesses to me that she has a small hole in her head through which things necessary to remember sometimes escape. Very inconvenient that little hole can be. Needless to say, to-day is a *jour de fête*. It always seems to be a Saint's Day when we run out of butter, or milk, or other vital things, and then, of course, all the shops are shut, and the only hope left to us is that some kindly peasant neighbour, remembering the holiday (for to him it means a ' bean-feast '), may have laid in a double store of provisions to entertain his friends.

One day I shall learn which of the saints are important enough to paralyse the commercial activities of the neighbouring town. I look through my French calendar and every blessed date seems to be dedicated to some saint or other, most of whom are utterly unknown to me.

Saint Arnoux, for instance ; who would have thought that his saintliness could upset one's daily life ? I had never heard of him before

Hilaire one day informed me that the next day would be the *Fête de St Arnoux*, and asked for leave to attend the pilgrimage to his shrine and the great ' peekaneek ' afterwards. This meant that Madame would feed the livestock and attend to Hilaire's various duties.

Asking as to St Arnoux, I could only gather that the peasants flock from miles around to join in the annual pilgrimage to the shrine of the Saint down in the Gorges du Loup. I was informed that a priest preaches a sermon in the open air, and that afterwards the multitude perch in clumps on various huge rocks in and about the mountain stream and eat their *déjeuner* of garlic, cheese, bread and wine sociably, if, as it sounded, uncomfortably. That part of the ceremony over, they all trail down to the hamlet below to join the younger and less pious members of the community who are already dancing in the open Square where the festivities continue till the small hours.

I had at once a desire to see the little shrine on the brink of the mountain torrent, and I resolved to avoid the *jour de fête*. And so the other day, leaving my car in the Square below, I walked up the mountain road bordering the Gorge until I came upon a narrow track leading down through sparse trees to the River Loup far below. I slid and scrambled down, picking the loveliest flowers, hepaticas, golden broom and wild veronica, amid the fissures of the great rocks as I descended,

" *About the mountain stream and eat their* déjeuner."

until suddenly at the very edge of the roaring mountain torrent dashing over great grey boulders, I came upon a tiny chapel built upon the rocks.

The *grille* was locked, but I peered through the bars into the damp gloom within where one hopeful candle flickered near the altar. Above it was the unfamiliar statue of a bearded man, presumably St Arnoux. On the walls were hung pathetic little souvenirs : a stained cotton glove ; several crudely modelled ships in glass cases upon rude shelves ; a handkerchief ; a leather belt. I wished that I knew the story of each and why it was placed there. On the floor were a few coins thrown through the *grille* by the devout for the benefit of the visiting priest and his poor. I threw in a shining ten-franc piece and a branch of blossoming broom, and then read the simple prayers to St Arnoux pencilled upon the outside walls of the chapel : pleas for the recovery of relations ; thanks for homely benefits conferred ; names of the affianced scrawled within hearts which in places seemed to have burst with emotion. After a while I descended worn stone steps over which some hidden spring gushed forth and cascaded downwards, losing itself in a grotto tunnelled under the foundations of the shrine itself. Hewn out of the wall was a stoup for Holy Water, filled eternally from the selfsame spring.

Suddenly I came out into an open space at the very edge of the torrent and was confronted with a tragic, lonely figure hanging upon a great wooden cross set upon a boulder in mid-stream. The beauty of it struck me into stillness. The

" That lonely Calvary."

211

figure of The Christ was carved in rough unpolished wood, but the carving was the work of an artist ; the anatomy of those pain-wracked limbs was perfect, as was that anguished look of suffering, of tenderness, of ineffable patience in the eyes of the strong, brave face.

Below the great cross swirled the mountain torrent ; on either side of it and lowering above it were dark, frowning mountains with wind-torn trees clinging for life to the bare face of the rock. The desolation of the place and the pathos of that Calvary in this wild and desolate Gorge affected me strongly, and when, at last, I turned away I felt it to be heartless to leave that gallant figure hanging there alone.

It was startling, that abrupt encounter, but very good for me because—until then—I had been feeling tragic and lonely too.

Back in my Domaine, my imagination filled with the beauty of that lonely Calvary and the shrine of St Arnoux, I questioned Emilia next morning about the Saint. Airily whisking her feather brush (which I notice is becoming bald so rapidly that it must be replaced), she replied—

" *Je ne sais pas, Madame, mais je crois qu'on m'a dit qu'il a tué son père et sa mère.*" (" I do not know, Madame, but I think I was told that he killed his father and mother.")

I was so staggered by this unexpected answer that I dared ask no further questions.

As Hilaire had had his ' jolly ' on the Fête de St Arnoux, I took Emilia with me to that of *St Jean de Malbosc*, the Saint of our own particular district. She was equally vague as to the history of St Jean, but she was quite certain that the peasants' ball given in his honour would be amusing. We drove down in great state in my car ; Emilia, a little blonde cousin of mine who was staying with us at the time, and Madame, who was, of course, the chauffeuse. Monsieur, who had a book to review, preferred to read it in peace in his *Galerie*.

Emilia wore a marvellous jumper of tooth-powder pink, and was so excited that she could hardly sit still. As we descended our mountain we could see, through the olive groves, the great lit tent in which the dancing was taking place, glowing in the darkness, and hear the strains of the pip-squeak local band floating up to us.

We were received by the Committee who had arranged the *Fête*—a deputation of callow youths with buttonholes of Brobdingnagian proportions and heads which appeared to have been dipped into the family *estagnon* of olive oil, so brightly did they shine in the light of the lanterns swinging above them.

To the strains of the pip-squeak band.

Every inhabitant of the *quartier*, men, women, and children, seemed to be packed into that big tent. Young men and maidens were revolving rhythmically to the hellish din evoked by the local musicians. Papas and mammas sat stiffly in rows upon hard wooden chairs and benches, talking to each other out of the corners of their mouths, far too self-conscious in their best clothes to turn and comfortably confront each other. Children skipped and raced between the legs of the dancers and under the guy-ropes of the tent, sucking oranges and sweet-sticks and licking cornets of ice-cream. The atmosphere simply hit one in the eye. I tried to analyse the smells. Garlic, and the odour of human exertion, of course, predominated ; but there were under-currents of peppermint, oranges, aniseed, vanilla, black Italian cheroot, Caporal cigarettes, sawdust, paraffin, hot broadcloth and cheap scent, jasmin and carnation in the ascendant. Then my sense of smell became paralysed and I could, perhaps fortunately, distinguish no more.

Emilia, only just out of mourning for some distant relative, refused to dance, though I gathered that she would have sung if asked. She sat by my side humming the tunes, her little fat feet tapping against the floor in time to the music ; her eyes sparkling, her buzzle-head in its saucy *béret* nodding to her numerous acquaintances. Occasionally I felt a sharp dig in the ribs from her elbow (incredibly sharp from so plump and rounded an elbow) as some entranced couple gyrated past us, and an excited whisper of names and probabilities was hissed into my ear.

My little cousin was all agog to dance with the youth of the village, and after I had shaken the hands of a few of the workmen who had helped to enlarge our Domaine, some shy advances were made and introductions effected. I could see that these dark *Provencaux* were mad to dance with the little blonde English *Mademoiselle*. Well— why not ?

Of course, she had the time of her life. She was not familiar with many of the queer steps introduced by her partners, and her sandalled feet pattered about upon hobnailed boots, *sabots*, and *espadrilles ;* but her halting French, stammered with an appalling English accent, her round pink baby face, gay blue eyes, blonde hair and schoolgirl laughter, had a *succès fou*.

Madame longed to dance, but sadly realised that in the forties one becomes a chaperone. Murmuring this into Emilia's sympathetic ear, Madame was assured that the son of the carpenter had remarked to Emilia that Madame was ' *belle comme un cœur*,' and that all present longed to

dance with her but would never have the courage
to ask such an honour. Madame, well accustomed
to her Emilia's pleasant blandishments, winked
a mental eye and essayed conversation with a
puce-faced matron planted on her other side,
covered with clinging children as a rock is
garnished with limpets.

In the interval, while the orchestra refreshed
itself with wine, Madame had an idea. Inactive
life has never attracted her, and the gaiety around
her effervesced in her blood like yeast in ginger-
beer. She would collect the superfluous children
who had been maddening the dancers by dodging
between them, and they would have an organised
romp.

Detaching a handful from the perspiring matron
by her side, she ran into the centre of the tent,
clutching more children as she ran, who in their
turn seized the hands of others until a great
uproarious ring of children was formed who
danced and sang around the centre pole. Then
Madame led a laughing, shouting, singing procession of babies in a mad ' Follow my Leader '
dance round the tent, black eyes dancing, dark
curls tossing, fat little legs and arms waving and
gesticulating, shrill treble voices piping and chanting until, when the music began again and the
river of children flowed outward to the waiting

benches which surrounded the tent, Madame sank into a chair exhausted, and her followers were too hot and breathless to have any further desire to run among the dancers and so impede their progress.

After that, Madame became the rock to which the limpets clung, and the rest of her evening was pure joy.

We all drove home in the summer moonlight amid the heavy scent of dew-wet flowers (very refreshing after the odours of that tent), chattering of our experiences. Emilia brewed us some glorious China tea when we got home before we tumbled into bed. So ended the *Fête de Saint Jean de Malbosc*.

But there is another even more picturesque *fête*, of the great St Jean, when every hamlet and every peasant proprietor lights a huge bonfire at night. Seen from my Provençal tower which overlooks a vast panorama of olive groves and rounded mountains stretching down to the encircling sea, the scene is magically beautiful. Dusk enfolds it, and the mountains become mighty and mysterious, and then, suddenly, a blaze of orange light on the dark peak of a hill, and the first bonfire is lit. Gradually, on every little hill and every towering peak, flame forth these fiery beacons, their scarlet-and-orange flames leaping up into the night sky, illuming little Provençal homesteads, glittering upon their windows and lighting up tall pointed cypresses standing dark and gaunt against the skyline.

Knowing the Provençal customs, one's imagination pictures the rest. Round each great fire peasants are clustered, old and young alike feeding the flames; each hamlet vying with its neighbour in making the grandest fire, the most conspicuous beacon. The young people must jump across it before the flames become too fierce and high, for this brings good luck to the men and early and satisfactory marriage to the maidens. No one can tell me why or whence this superstition arose, nor can I gather the reason why St Jean and also St Pierre should be honoured in this fiery and picturesque manner on their respective *fête* days.

Hilaire promised me a bonfire last year, but in the end could not resist the attraction of the huge, communal beacon piled higher up the mountain. His excuse for his desertion was that our garden was so full of flowers and vines and fruit-trees and olive-trees that we could not make an adequate bonfire without damaging our growing things with its flames. So Madame rushed forth in the car and bought a handful of rockets and Roman candles, which she fired from the roof-terrace to the increasing agony of Monsieur down below, who dissociated himself vigorously from the display and was convinced that she would certainly blow up either herself, the house—or both. She did neither, and thoroughly enjoyed this lively little hell of her own making, hoping earnestly that her peasant neighbours got as much joy out of it as she did.

In France "The Little Flower" — *Sainte Thèrese de L'Enfant Jésus*—is perhaps the most loved of all the saints in the Calendar, particularly by the children; perhaps because she died so young and they think that she understands their childish troubles and petitions and will not laugh at them. She is always represented with a spray of roses in her hands because of her prayer that, after death, she might be allowed to bring comfort to the sad, the sick, and the desolate, and that, through her constant intercession, blessings might fall upon mankind like *une pluie des roses* (a rain of roses).

Having been given a lovely statue of "The Little Flower" for my rose-garden, duly blessed by the village priest, I decided to have a little *Fête* for the children in the Domaine upon the Feast Day of *Sainte Thèrese*, and I chose two grubby dark-eyed maidens to run round with my invitations.

On the day itself we were much perturbed by

threatening clouds which obscured the sun and
foretold a thunderstorm. I had invited my small
guests to come at three o'clock, give their flowers
to *Sainte Thèrese*, and then drink hot chocolate
and eat *brioches* and *bon-bons* with Madame.

During luncheon the storm broke. Rivers of
blue lightning streamed down the lightning-conductor of the Tower, and the noise of the thunder
was deafening. Huge hailstones rattled down
upon the flowers and tore their petals into shreds.
It was short and sharp, that thunderstorm, but
everything in the garden was soaked and I feared
that our little *Fête* was spoiled. We were staring
drearily out at the wreckage in the garden, when
I suddenly became aware of four small boys
peering into the *Galerie* with their noses pressed
against the glass door at the end of it.

It was then only one o'clock, but I realised with
dismay that the first of my guests had arrived.
One o'clock for three o'clock is a trifle early, and
so I opened the door and told them that the
Fête would not begin for two hours and that
I had not yet had time to arrange anything.
Whereupon, instead of running away, my four
urchins all volunteered to help me with the
preparations.

Seeing that their hands were full of a motley
assortment of flowers I suggested that as the

storm had ceased they should first go round to the rose-garden and make their offerings to *Sainte Thèrese* and then come back to help me to transform the garage into a tea-room.

From an upper window I watched the boys rollick round the house and race down into the rose-garden until they reached the little Saint standing, white and pure, between the dark cypresses. There they stopped abruptly, pulled off their ragged caps, crossed themselves and stood bare-headed, silent before her beauty.

Then they began to decorate the statue. One small boy climbed up and timidly placed a sceptre of ' Love-Lies-Bleeding ' in her hand ; another tucked a rose into the folds of her coif so that it touched her cheek. They were alone together and had no idea that I was watching them, but I could see that " The Little Flower " was a very real personality to them.

Soon they came back to me and helped me to fix up benches and to carry out cups and saucers to the garage, the garden being too drenched for the open air feast that I had planned ; and gradually more guests began to appear. These were of all sizes, ages and shapes. Fat brown babies, very scantily attired, carried in the arms of elder sisters who were dressed in mother's old skirt, looped up into panniers at each side ;

smarter maidens in fashionable though cheap clothes ; dark-eyed, bullet-headed boys ; a few

Decorating Sainte Thèrese.

little brides clad in their white *Première Communion* robes, and all of them carrying large bunches of flowers.

We had imagined that the rain would prevent most of the children from coming, because many of them lived in isolated parts either high up or low down in the mountains, so that, to reach the Domaine, they must make a painful ascent or descent over mountain tracks and through dripping olive groves. But a large party of little pilgrims appeared, some of them drenched to the skin, but all eager to lay their flowers at the feet of *Sainte Thérèse*. She was completely embowered in them when the offerings were all given, and only her lovely little head emerged above the sea of blossom.

The children had a lovely *Fête*, and Emilia and Lucienne, aided by Madame Hilaire and neighbouring mammas, brewed countless jugs of steaming chocolate for our small guests. Hilaire was the only person who did not enjoy it. Of course, I invited him to be present, as a member of our small staff, but I believe that he was thoroughly miserable all the time, fearing damage to his beloved garden. He even looked disappointed next day when he failed to find that his apprehensions were well founded.

Every village has its own individual patron saint and its own particular *fête*. The whole summer is peppered with them, as I know to my cost, for my giddy *femme-de-chambre* (lately suppressed because it is absurd for one lone woman to be waited upon by two others) was obsessed with the desire to dance and knew her cursed calendar by heart.

When Lucienne's long French nose appeared round the door and her face followed, irradiated with an ingratiating smile, Madame knew perfectly well that permission was about to be asked for another ' jolly.' Emilia, always unselfish, readily did Lucienne's work and allowed her to go gadding —*if* Madame consented, and Madame, having an inconvenient sympathy for youth, and love, and dancing, generally did.

But on the great universal *Fête* days everyone has a holiday and everyone takes part. I well remember *Le Fête-Dieu* last year. Emilia persuaded me to drive Monsieur to the ancient town near-by to watch the procession from the shop window of a kindly tradesman. In his doorway was to be set up a wayside altar. By this we should be partially screened, and, in the darkness of the shop behind it, could see without being seen, and Monsieur, who had but lately recovered from a long illness, could be comfortably ensconced in a big arm-chair and be refreshed with tea before the homeward journey. So we decided to go.

Bells were clanging, chiming and tolling from every tower and steeple as we approached the old town. There was no rhythm in their ringing but just a joyous din, as though each sweating Provençal ringer in every stuffy belfry were vying with his comrades to see who could make the loudest noise for the greater glory of God.

" Bells were clanging."

From every old balcony of beautifully hand-wrought iron (the great industry of our town) hung white bed coverlets, hand-quilted in intricate designs of flowers and birds, and each flower and bird laboriously stuffed with wool or cotton to give a raised effect. These Provençal bed - quilts are very beautiful and are only brought forth on great occasions. Some are edged with real lace, some with heavily embroidered mull ; all are delicate, lovely and ancient ; heirlooms every one and prized possessions. They hung out like banners over our heads and waved gently in the breeze above the narrow streets.

We parked the car and proceeded on foot, knowing that the streets, so narrow that the wheels of a car scrape the kerbstone, would be densely packed with people. We were enchanted with the scene. Here and there, under an old archway, in a narrow angle of a street, the porch of a church or the doorway of a shop, white altars had been set up covered with lovely stuffs; massed with flowers, roses and carnations, lilies, and great sprays of the scented Spanish broom which riots wild upon the mountains of Provence in the early summer, the scented profusion lit by hundreds of candles. Behind these altars were stretched white linen sheets, with real roses and carnations sewn singly upon them, giving a lovely jewelled effect, so simply gained. On the steps of the shrines were posed little white-clad children with crowns upon their heads and angels' wings of pale blue transparent gauze sewn upon their shoulders, their hands clasped in an attitude of prayer. Very theatrical but quite charming. They remained perfectly still as the crowd passed them and strewed flowers upon the altar steps.

Fearing that Monsieur would overtire himself by climbing those tortuous streets of cobbled stones, I suggested that we should now take shelter in the hospitable shop and watch the scene from there.

Hardly had we settled into our places when

there was a sudden silence in the streets without. The bells ceased and expectant faces all turned one way. Just at this moment a tiny baby boy, clad in a skimpy white shirt, a wreath of roses worn crookedly over one eye, detached himself from his mother and waddled unsteadily, like a baby Bacchus, across the main street to admire his own reflection in a shop window opposite. Monsieur twinkled, and the crowd laughed softly at the antics of this very human cherub.

There was a sound of distant chanting, and the waiting people flattened themselves against the houses to make room for the coming procession. And suddenly, at the top of one of the narrowest and most precipitous streets, directly in our line of vision, where the gables of old houses lean across and almost touch each other, appeared outlined against the sky the black figure of the Cathedral sacristan flanked by little scarlet acolytes. In his hands he held the ends of two white ribbons to which clung a flock of white-clad flower-crowned baby girls who toddled at his heels in two parallel lines. Being too young to be drilled, they had been placed at regular intervals one behind the other, one hand clinging to the stretched ribbon while the other clutched a miniature basket of flower-petals to throw upon the altars as they passed.

Behind them followed a mass of little white brides who had lately received their *Première Communion*, walking with quiet dignity in their long white dresses and flowing veils held in place by wreaths of white flowers. As each altar was passed, all turned towards it, and as we were seated in a dark window flanking the largest altar in the town, we could watch these little upturned faces without being seen. We looked into eyes black, brown, amber, blue, and grey ; the innocent eyes of children, bright with the reflected glitter of the altar candles. We saw small hands making the sign of the cross and scattering blossoms about the shrine. One tiny boy, desiring evidently to make quite sure that *le bon Dieu* really did get his flowers, broke loose from the procession, climbed the altar steps, and standing on tiptoe, stretched up and laid his gift upon the altar itself—some weary little wild flowers — before being swept away in the receding flood of children.

It flowed down the steep incline in full sunshine, growing in volume every moment. Here were the youthful members of the *Société des Mimosas* in their long white gowns slashed across with scarves of golden silk and yellow fillets binding their white veils. After them came the orphans of *Sainte Marthe* in sky blue. Next the girl Crusaders in white tabards worn over blue tunics with huge pale blue crosses sewn from chin to knee ; and then hundreds of schoolgirls of all ages dressed in white, shepherded by quiet nuns.

Dividing the stream of girls from the advancing boys walked a priest with a brown, rugged face. His personality arrested one immediately. A by-stander whispered to us that this priest merits well the name of ' Father,' for he has won the heart of every child in the town and to-day more than a thousand follow him.

One could see his influence in the faces of the crowd of boys behind him. Those who had taken their *Première Communion* that year were dressed as sailors with white collars, long blue trousers, flat round caps, huge white streamers and bows tied to their left arms, and small mother-of-pearl crucifixes slung by white ribbons around their necks. Mothers who could not afford to buy a sailor suit for their boys had gained the same effect by folding a white cloth cornerways and tucking it into the collar of an ordinary blue suit.

Monsieur deplored to me the fact that there was no attempt to make the boys march in formation as there would have been in orderly England. The boys just raced and tumbled over each other, but I could see that it was their desire to keep as near as possible to their beloved priest that caused the disorder, and therefore I rather liked it.

Hard on their heels scrambled a rabble of untidy children, wearing no distinctive dress, sons and daughters of lazy or unbelieving parents whom yet the priest has, by his personal magnetism, drawn into his flock. It seems that there is no reason save indifference for neglect of personal appearance on this great day, for the benevolent of the town, the school teachers, and the nuns are always ready to provide suitable apparel for the little ones for *Le Fête-Dieu*.

These ragged followers had evidently broken loose from parental restriction, and, as they paused with their priest beside a wayside altar, they stared up at him, wide-eyed, and repeated in shrill voices his little Litany of the Commonplace.

I loved his simple Litany. He prayed that God would protect all children and bless their homes, their parents and their work. One heard the short sentences repeated in various octaves down the narrow street, rising from deep bass to piercing treble as the crowd and the children followed him through all the humble prayers.

Then the flood rolled on. More children, more banners, more priests, and then a crowd of grown-up people in which we recognised our small domestic staff.

Last of all, a proud, white banner heralded the Bishop who carried the Host. He blessed the altars, the people, the flowers. The air became thick with floating blossoms of golden broom showered from upper windows. Then followed the sonorous Corpus Christi hymn, which was caught up by the joyful crowd and rang and vibrated triumphantly through old arches and narrow streets as the procession, now completely encircling the town, wound slowly through them on its way to the Cathedral.

We all drew a deep breath, and then our kindly friends suggested that we should go upstairs to the equivalent of the English best parlour (and not unlike it) to drink those promised cups of tea. This we gratefully did, and when I had eaten a sticky Provençal cake, I left Monsieur enjoying a quiet cigarette and was taken up to the top of the old house to see the view from the roof.

A wonderful old staircase we climbed, and arrived, winded, at the top. Then our host's daughter led me through a queer, drunken arch in the wall, and I found myself upon a little balcony which had been transformed into a miniature garden. Twenty-three varieties of flowers were growing up there in the sky in a space not five feet by four. Sweet-peas and Morning Glory convolvulus ramped up bamboo canes ; fat zinnias, purple-and-white fuchsias, pansies, pinks, and violas, even a tiny rose-tree was there in bloom. Below us lay a jumble of crazy, crooked roofs and gables, tiled with the old Provençal split drain-pipe tiles, weathered to grey, ochre, and rose-colour ; and the tower of the Cathedral which is over a thousand years old.

I stood entranced ; it was a sight that would have delighted the eye of Hollar, that specialist in crooked roofs, and I longed for Monsieur to be able to enjoy it too, and sadly knew that such an ascent would be quite impossible for him.

We drove back to our Domaine to find it dozing in the afternoon sunlight, embowered in flowers. But I realised, amusedly, that our garden lacked many of the varieties that I had just seen blooming upon a tiny balcony up in the sky.

Another delightful *fête* was the Fragonard anniversary, which took place before Monsieur fell ill. I had been in England and reached home an hour before the procession was to take place in the town. Of course, I got the usual enthusiastic welcome from our little staff : Emilia throwing her fat little arms round Madame's neck and plant-ing a smacking kiss upon either cheek, Lucienne dancing about excitedly, and Hilaire, his old bald head bared and shining in the sun, nearly shaking my hand off. In the background stood the tall, slim figure of Monsieur, the characteristic eyeglass screwed into his brilliant deep-set eye, watching it all with a beaming smile, knowing that his turn would come. It did.

Then I told Hilaire to haul out my luggage, seized a suit-case which I knew contained a clean frock; rushed upstairs shouting to my servants to put on their hats, and did a quick change myself.

I bundled Monsieur and the staff into the car, and in a quarter of an hour we were all lined up along the pavement in the centre of the town, gay with festoons of flowers hanging from scarlet-painted poles, and we waited for the pageant to begin.

To the delight of Hilaire, it started with the firing of a big gun followed by the sound of queer distant music, and presently a band of players appeared playing old Provençal instruments. These men were all wearing the dress of Fragonard's day and looked picturesque though unbeautifully hot. Behind them came delicious girls wearing *coifs* with shallow, shady Provençal straw hats perched above them and tied under the chin with ribbons. They rode upon pillioned horses decorated with favours, and in some cases two little girls shared one horse.

Fragonard's representative appeared in a painted coach (lent by the Fragonard Museum), and as he drove along with his patrons he waved greetings to friends who, dressed in the costume of the period, were stationed in the windows and balconies of the actual houses in which those people once lived. The pageant was beautifully dressed and arranged, but I got even more enjoyment from the bystanders, my staff included, who kept on recognising friends and relatives in the garb of Fragonard's patrons and followers, and who did not attempt to hide their delight and excitement, making desperate efforts to attract the attention of the actors.

Emilia at once spied her small niece, mounted upon a noble steed which, as Hilaire loudly explained, was the property of his friend the blacksmith. There followed, of course, the whole histories both of the little niece who had had a spot on her nose and could hardly be persuaded to exhibit herself to-day, *pauvre petite*, and of the blacksmith who, I was informed, had kidney trouble and suffered agonies whilst plying his trade.

I caught Lucienne ogling a good-looking youth in a frogged satin coat, one of the patrons of Fragonard, and was instantly told by Emilia that he was a *coiffeur*, with his own business in a neighbouring village, and much *épris* with Lucienne. This explained to me the wonder of Lucienne's permanently *chic* and shingled head.

Hilaire spotted one of his Chasseur Alpin sons among the soldiery, and I was told that his officer had allowed him an afternoon's leave in order that he might fire off the old cannon (whose report we had just heard) from the Fragonard Museum. His father hoped that *le petit* would be allowed to come home to his mother for his supper because the food in barracks was not equal to that supplied at home. I noticed no signs of starvation in the full-moon face of Hilaire's offspring, but I listened, sympathetically I hope, to the *régime* of military diet.

At the most impressive moment of the pageant, suddenly a wild squealing was heard, and I saw a man approaching from whom these sounds presumably emanated. As he passed me I saw that he was wearing a small sucking pig round his neck like a fichu, its legs tied together under his chin and its poor fat little body forming a roll-collar at the back of his neck. Hilaire enviously explained that the pig had been won in a lottery that afternoon—some people had all the luck. Hilaire himself had put in for two tickets, one for himself and another for his wife, but he never won fat sucking pigs, not he—and all his family adored pork. Gloom descended upon him like a fog.

I rushed into a neighbouring café and bought him a packet of his favourite Caporal cigarettes as a consolation prize, and some bon-bons for Lucienne and Emilia ; then, the procession being over, I tucked my party into the car and drove them home smoking and sucking contentedly. I was very tired after my night journey in the train, but well pleased to have arrived home in time to give my little people their long-anticipated treat.

More elaborate and sophisticated are the festivals of the Coast ; the early Carnivals of the spring ; the processions of flower-decked cars followed by the battles of flowers—which can be extremely painful. A friend of mine once rashly decorated her car and took part in a procession, but when the battle of flowers began, her poor face became so bruised, being pelted with the heads of carnations and roses from which, both hands being occupied with the steering-wheel and gear-levers, she was unable to protect herself, that she never repeated the experience. When I was taken to my first Carnival I was naturally very much excited. My hostess drove a party of us to the illuminated town where the whole population was dancing down by the sea. It was a very pretty sight because everyone was in fancy dress, whirling about under the umbrella-shaped

plane - trees upon which were hung myriads of
round red-and-yellow Chinese lanterns. Fire-
works shot up from the quay and were reflected
in the quiet waters of the harbour, and the old
town with its ancient Cathedral perched upon
steep rocks above us, was beautifully flood-lit in
the way that only the French really understand.

The girls of our party were, I knew, longing to
get out of the car and dance among the mad
crowd, chaperoned by me ; but my spirit quailed
when I saw that the chief amusement on these
occasions is for the men of the town to join hands
and then form a ring around any pretty girl of
their selection, who is not allowed to escape until
she has paid forfeit of a kiss all round. None of
our party was masked or in fancy dress, so would
be all the more conspicuous. The girls were all
pretty blondes, and I knew that if they were once
let loose in that excitable Southern mob I should
never find them again till next morning. It was
then suggested that the stolid English chauffeur
should accompany us for our protection, but
hardly had this suggestion been made when he
was nearly torn from the driver's seat by a bevy
of pretty laughing girls, one of whom, leaping on
to the seat beside him, flung her arms around
his neck and kissed him upon both cheeks. I
found that the girls of the town had started the

same wild game as the men, and I felt that the good-looking English chauffeur would not long be allowed to act as our bodyguard.

As compensation, we were driven along the edge of the harbour where a Venetian *Fête* was in progress. The English gun-boats anchored there were illuminated from bows to stern with coloured electric lights, and their searchlights played about the mountains and the sea. All the small boats were festooned with flowers and had a red Chinese lantern swinging from their bows. Their occupants, wearing fancy dress, sang as they drifted over the radiant water which reflected every light and colour as only the crystal-clear Mediterranean can.

We sat in the car watching the lovely scene until the last shower of rockets whizzed into the air and the last coloured spark fizzled in the harbour. Then Monsieur and I said good night and drove up into our mountains.

We found our little Domaine dreaming under the stars. Thousands of fireflies were flitting among the flowers, lighting each blossom into colour as they passed. Down amid the olive groves they flickered in the green gloom like tiny electric sparks. Glow-worms burned little green lights from the old grey walls, and the air throbbed with the song of nightingales.

I stopped the engine of the car and switched off the lights, and for a time Monsieur and I sat in stillness gazing and listening. After a while he turned to me and said—

" This is better than the works of man, Sweetheart."

THE HARVESTS.

MONSIEUR and I had always been childishly excited over a yield of any kind in our homes. Never
shall I forget the thrill of finding the first egg from
our intensive hens which we housed upon the
tiny roof-garden of a small house in London
during the war. At the sound of the first con-
ceited cackle of a hen, Monsieur dashed from his
garden-study where he was writing military history
and tore upstairs, jostling the cook who thundered
up from her basement, and the house-parlourmaid
who came scudding from an upper flight, and
eventually colliding with me as I shot from the
drawing-room, all of us eager to be the first in
the finding of that wonderful egg.

Later, in our Hampstead garden, there was
the excitement of counting our cherry crop (the
maximum yield was nine cherries), and our few
apples, and of taking the temperature every half-
hour of our precious William pear ; for everyone
knows that it is vital to sit up all night with a
William pear that is upon the point of ripening,
lest the precise moment for picking it be lost and
it become a mere potato.

So that when we came to live in Provence and took possession of a little domaine, stocked with melons, apricots, figs, greengages, cherries, strawberries, peaches, its terraces lined with fruitful vines and also a grove of olive-trees, we lived in a series of thrills as crop after crop ripened and must be harvested.

The olive crop came first, and I awoke one morning to the sound of a curious intermittent tapping, as though hundreds of woodpeckers were at work in the woods below the house. To satisfy my curiosity, I leaped out of bed, rushed to a window, and peered out. I saw a sea of grey-green foliage rippling into silvery waves as the mistral swept over it, and under this sea the gnarled trunks of a myriad olive-trees. Up in the tossing boughs, sometimes submerged by waves of foliage, sometimes silhouetted against the bluest sky in the world, were men shouting and laughing. Each man clung to his tree with his left arm, while with his right, holding a long bamboo, he beat the branches. I realised that the olive harvest had begun, and that all our peasant neighbours were already out in the sunshine gathering their crops.

I roused Monsieur, who was as eager as I to pick our own olives and to use our own olive oil; and, when we had drunk our coffee, taking the

advice of Emilia, we dressed ourselves in workmen's ancient overalls (because the juice of olive
leaves a permanent stain), and went out into the
garden to find Hilaire.

He was childishly keen to pick olives and to
give us a demonstration of his skill in climbing
trees, and at once went in search of a long bamboo
and the curious ladder, made like the spine of a
Dover sole, such as all the Provençaux use. Our
two little maids also were delighted to leave
their work indoors and join us in the olive
grove.

While they fetched sacks and sheets to spread
under the trees to catch the fruit and Hilaire
searched for his bamboo, Monsieur and I walked
across to our neighbour's terraces to watch him
and his family harvesting their crop. They were
all there : father, mother, sons, daughters, grand-
parents, and grandchildren. The men were up
in the trees, and the women, children, and old
people were picking up the olives, which rattled
down through the leaves in a purple-black hail
and fell and bounced upon the sacks and sheets,
also upon the backs and heads beneath.

A yell of " *Mefiez-vous ! Mefiez-vous !* " from
the men above heralded each shower of fruit,
and we watched the big wooden measures being
filled incredibly quickly, the damaged fruit and

broken and rotten twigs (purposely knocked off to clean the trees) being thrown aside.

Emilia joined us, and at once poured into my ear a stream of romantic gossip. I was asked to observe a bright-eyed girl with an orange hand-kerchief tied over her black curls, who, to Emilia's scorn, had started at the foot of the mountain and was climbing slowly upward. Only a novice would do that, Emilia explained ; women who are accustomed to the back-breaking toil of collecting olives start at the top of a slope and creep gradually downwards. Also a true Pro-vençale would never be foolish enough to wear a dainty lace apron (already indelibly stained, as the pretty girl will find) for such work. But she is a *femme-de-chambre* from a great house in Paris who has come south for the season with her mistress and has been invited by peasant relations to help them with their olive harvest. Emilia hinted that the girl was ' *très coquette,*' and had arrayed herself thus unsuitably for the sole purpose of attracting the men in the olive-trees. Even as she spoke I noticed the slim young Parisienne signalling to a dark muscular giant above her head beating the branches with a bare brown arm. His blue eyes looked dangerous, and I felt inclined to take up the peasant cry of ' *Mefiez-vous !* ' But after all it was their affair.

A minor howl from Hilaire of "MADAME-E-E-E!" recalled us to our own property, and our work began. Hilaire performed marvels of agility for a man of his age, and I hardly dared to watch him. I started collecting my olives in English fashion, picking them up with one hand and filling the other before throwing them into the measure, until gently corrected by Emilia, who gave me a swift and supple demonstration with ten stumpy but agile fingers all working at once : *" Il faut les ramasser avec les deux mains, Madame."*

I sadly watched her scudding about, her small fat feet heedlessly crushing the tiny delicate blue Roman hyacinths, small scarlet tulips, and big mauve anemones which carpet the terraces in spring, and I could not withhold a mild protest.

" Sont sauvages, Madame," replied Emilia, intent upon her olive crop. My attention wandered for a time, for that miracle of wild flowers was new to me. Had we not imported bulbs from Holland at great expense and spent hours in planting them in our garden ? and here in Provence, Nature had lavishly provided them duty-free !

Monsieur, close at hand, worked with his usual tremendous concentration. In all his work, like Cromwell's soldiers, he 'made some conscience' of what he did, and even Hilaire used to say, *" Monsieur travaille avec conscience."* He was determined that his olive oil should be of the first quality, and Hilaire often paused in his thrashing of the trees to wipe a beaming face with his hand, peer down at us through the leaves, and voice his approval.

Children danced about among the wild-flowers and pelted each other with olives—a sin which,

" *When the mistral blows, nerves are on edge.*"

had the mistral not been blowing, could not have passed unrebuked. But when the mistral blows, nerves are on edge and children over-excited. It is common knowledge that children must not be scolded during a mistral—*Mefiez-vous !*

We worked for our olive crop until evening came and our mountains were dyed rose-red in the sunset.   Cypress-trees stood out like dark sentinels against the glowing sky and the distant sea was veiled in a lilac mist.   One could no longer see to work, and the men threw down their long bamboos and came sliding and climbing down the tree-trunks and ladders, laughing and congratulating each other on a good day's work as the women and children clustered round them.

We watched them all stumbling heavy laden down the mountain path, the handsome giant contriving to find a free arm to support the steps of the pretty Parisienne ;   the older peasants calculating the weight of their crop, some of them grumbling and gesticulating.   Hilaire explained that in these modern days everyone has to pay a small fee for the services of the olive mill to crush the olives, and that this, since the owner keeps all the dregs of the oil and the pulp of the olives as his perquisite, seems unjust.   For the residue makes good *savon noir* (the equivalent of the English soft soap), which the French use for all cleaning purposes.   From the amount of this commodity used in our house, I should imagine that we are supporting several owners of mills.

To the great disappointment of Monsieur, our olives did not fill sixteen measures, and therefore our crop was not considered worthy of being crushed separately.   We were told that we could

either sell our olives at the mill, exchange them
for the equivalent in oil, or mix our crop with
that of a neighbour to make up the required
amount. This we did, and, from the musty flavour
of our share of the resulting oil, our neighbour
evidently had not worked 'with conscience,' but
had mixed mouldy and damaged fruit with the
good olives. However, we had enjoyed the olive
harvest and the visit to the old mill, and we
resolved to prune our neglected olive-trees to let
the sunlight into the centres and so get a better
crop the following year.

The flower harvests also have become family
affairs, since the scent factories can now afford
to pay so little for the flowers that the peasant
proprietors find hired help impossible. First there
is the violet harvest in February and March,
when all the terraces under the olive-trees are blue
and purple with blossom. My little staff picked
violets for two solid hours on my upper terrace
this year, and one day we sent away a huge market
basket filled with bunches and put six or seven
bowls of violets in every room. Even after that
it was impossible to see from where the blossoms
had been picked.

In April the air around the Domaine smells of
weddings, because the orange blossom is in full
bloom. My peasant neighbour grows orange

blossom and jessamine for market, and I wonder why I do not keep bees, for I should never have to feed them. His wife, a lady getting on in years, always presents me with a basket of the bitter wild oranges for marmalade when the flowers are over, and picks them herself. I regret to say that one day I found Hilaire in silent convulsions of laughter, and from his general appearance I knew that his mirth was unseemly. In answer to my questioning eyebrow, he pointed to my neighbour's terraces and whispered hoarsely that he had just seen old Madame Hippolyte climb up on to the slender branch of an orange tree, which, of course, broke beneath her weight, and she had fallen bump on her back and then rolled over the wall on to the terrace below (luckily only a shallow drop). In pantomime he described to me the manner in which she tumbled, and, from the way he suddenly enveloped his head in a sack and threw up his leg, I was left in no doubt but that the poor lady's skirts flew over her head as she fell.

Not a gleam of anxiety for his neighbour's fate did I see in Hilaire's eyes, and I strove to show the fitting concern which I really felt—and found it difficult. Why, in Provence, does one become so swiftly demoralised? The *gamine* in me grows more robust every day, and the gentlewoman that I hoped I was, more anæmic.

Next comes the rose harvest, and the fields in the valleys flame into a vivid pink. Only one variety of rose is cultivated for the scent industry, the *rose de Mai*, a shapeless rosette of exquisite perfume, whose petals are stripped from the calyx : an easier crop to harvest than the jessamine, because the bushes are higher and the work therefore is less back-breaking.

The jessamine crop, in August, is by far the most exhausting to gather, because of the intense heat. The majority of the peasants make up night parties, and work on until the sun rises and grows fierce. Driving back from some late festivity one meets them on their way to the jessamine fields ; sometimes carrying bobbing lanterns, the older peasants trudging doggedly along with an air of resignation ; the young ones sometimes dancing and singing, and the weary ones very often quietly weeping.

As in collecting olives, both hands are used to pluck the delicate flowers, which must never be bruised. It takes thousands upon thousands of little jessamine stars to fill a measure, and when I meet huge lorries [1] filled with them on the way

[1] In old days many of the women carried the baskets of blossom to the *Parfumerie* balanced on their heads, and, until quite lately, an old neighbour of mine could be seen marching to her market with a huge basket perched upon her head, and both hands busily engaged in knitting a striped stocking in the red and white colours of Provence.

to market and am almost intoxicated by the trail
of hot perfume left behind as I follow in my car,
I sometimes think of those tears of utter weariness
that have been shed upon them.

I also remember the fate of the sister of my
little *femme-de-chambre*, who was returning one
night through the dark fields dragging with her a
heavy basket of jessamine flowers. As she passed
under the eaves of some old buildings a great
snake fell from them and hung writhing for a
moment around her neck. The snake was a harmless kind and probably as terrified as she was,
but the shock and horror of it threw the poor
child into a fit, and for days the family feared for
her reason. Since then she has been subject to
fits and unable to work.

Personally I have never seen a snake in Provence,
and happily there are none in our little Paradise ;
but Hilaire, who goes up into the woods to cut
green stuff for the rabbits, tells me that he sees
many, all harmless, and that he runs after them
and cuts off their heads with his sickle. This
seems to me so extraordinary, for Hilaire is terrified
of mice, calls them *petits rats* (little rats), says
their bite is dangerous, and flees from them.
Yet he pursues snakes with cheerful vigour. Now
I am unafraid of mice, but the sight of an ordinary
garden worm sends a chill down my spine—and

the very thought of a snake——! I have always admired the courageous Eve for parleying with a serpent.

The lavender harvest, culled also for essential oils, is cut by men high up in the mountains, which, in July and August, are blue with wild lavender. Wanting to see—and smell—these men at work, I drove my car up into the heights one summer evening, and, leaving it in the square of a tiny village, continued the ascent on foot.

After I had climbed my selected mountain for some time, my nose was suddenly assailed by a strong perfume, not of lavender but of onion soup. This was so startling and unexpected that it brought me to a halt. I looked around me and could only see an ancient curved wall to my left, but my curiosity was aroused and I scrambled up to it and walked under a half-arch hung with ferns. Within the wall I found myself standing in a circular open space, and I saw a ruined shelter of rugged boulders leaning up against massive rocks, piled one upon another, cemented together with sand and clay which crumbled at a touch, and covered in with a picturesque sloping roof of weathered Provençal tiles.

From slits in this wall the smell of onion soup emanated, and I peered into a larger aperture which had once evidently been a door, and saw an old peasant stirring a pot over a handful of burning sticks. I hailed him cheerily, and told him that the smell of his good soup had attracted me there. He was obviously surprised and delighted to hear a human voice in the loneliness of the mountains, and he greeted me cordially, then, in the garrulous Provençal way, began to talk. He was camping in this lovely but desolate spot in order to cut lavender, and had found this ruin convenient. Would Madame care to enter it and look around her?

Of course, I eagerly accepted his invitation, and found myself in a fairly lofty place divided into three compartments by the same rugged walls, which were cut by half-arches like the one I had first passed through. The outside walls were pierced by slits among the boulders, and the dilapidated roof was supported by the boles of dead trees stretched across from rock to rock.

The old man told me that hundreds of years ago this had been a shepherd's hut; that the circular space outside was once used as a shelter for sheep when the mistral ravaged the pasturage, and that those curious slits in the walls were used by the shepherd to shoot arrows at marauding wolves. He reached up to one of the tree-boles in the roof and produced a piece of rusty iron of curious circular shape, and told me that this

" He greeted me cordially."

was an ancient wolf-trap that he had discovered
hidden there.

In such a place had David sheltered with his

sheep and sung his psalms. Outside were the high mountains, the refuge for the wild goats, and the rocks for the conies. Up there he would naturally feel that he had become as an owl of the waste places as he watched, and like a sparrow that is alone upon the housetop; and at night I was sure that all the beasts of the forest did creep forth.

There was even a spring in the valley running among the mountains, where that boy of ruddy and fair countenance could have found smooth stones for his sling and have amused his solitude by practising an art which would one day kill a tiresome giant.

My dream was interrupted by my old man, who suddenly produced a bundle of blue lavender spikes for Madame's acceptance, and she made him a grateful farewell and descended the mountain accompanied by the ghost of a shepherd lad who once found favour in the eyes of a capricious king.

The mountain lavender is so delicious that I have tried desperately to dig up a few plants for my rock garden, but the soil is so scanty among the rocks that the poor starved roots have to grow down until they reach Australia for nourishment, and none of my broken specimens has ever survived. This is very sad, for the garden variety

of lavender out here is entirely different from the
wild or English kinds. It has a feathery leaf,
which smells aromatic and 'herby' rather than
sweet, and its flowers are a deep and intense blue.
Our walls are full of it mixed with shocks of rose-
mary, which is characteristically Provençal, and
both plants seed themselves everywhere. But I
discovered this year that beneath our crop of
lavender and rosemary lurked a marvellous harvest
of snails. I have never seen so many snails in
my life of every size and shape, and Hilaire tells
me that they live in the crevices of the old walls
and come out regularly to take the evening air.

My sister and her little girl, who were staying
with me lately, decided to wage war upon snails
and rid my domaine of this pest. After a shower
of rain they started collecting the horrible things
in a small tin. In ten minutes they asked for a
bucket, and in half an hour it was nearly filled
with a mass of slimy crawling horror.

The problem then arose as to what we were to
do with the snails when collected, but Emilia,
happening to pass on her way to feed the chickens,
told us with glistening eyes that the large snails
were delicious to eat and that her brother-in-law
had a passion for them. Accordingly we presented her with the grisly bucket, and were then
informed that the snails must be left to starve

for a few days, during which time they would spit out all their poisons. After that there must follow a long process of cleaning and pickling before they could be eaten.

This was not at all what I had bargained for. I wanted to get rid of the beastly things at once, and for days on end we all went cold with disgust as we passed that sinister covered pail outside the kitchen door, and we all longed for Emilia's day-out to come, when she would carry it home to her brother-in-law, whose wife was to complete the preparation of the feast.

Thursday at last arrived, and Emilia assured me that she would take the snails home with her that afternoon while we were out for a picnic by the sea. When we returned in the evening the pail had disappeared, and for this we were all thankful; but one look at Emilia's face when I asked her about it told me that for some reason she had not taken those snails to the expectant brother-in-law. I wondered secretly in which corner of the Domaine she had thrown them, and hoped that they were too far gone to do much damage. For days I walked delicately, like Agag, in my garden, fearing to come upon that mass of horror; but I did not learn the truth until a month later.

I had been obliged through circumstances to

reduce my staff of two to only one, and Lucienne, my French *femme-de-chambre*, being the latest comer and in any case not comparable in any way to my faithful little Italian Emilia, who has been with us since we first came to Provence, was the obvious one to be economised away. In spite of excellent references from me, written both in French and in English, Lucienne was very sore over her dismissal, and bitterly resented the fact that Madame was keeping an Italian and dispensing with a Frenchwoman. Her spleen was not visited upon me but upon the innocent Emilia, whose life was made a misery by Lucienne's jealousy and reproaches.

I never realised what a pitch jealousy could reach in a southern climate until, long after the departure of Lucienne, Emilia, finding Madame once more intent upon the capture of snails, poured forth the story of that last sinister pailful.

It appeared that Emilia, having business in the town upon that fateful Thursday afternoon, realised that she could not carry a bucket full of snails with her to her appointment, and so offered its contents to the washerwoman who was working that day at the Domaine. The woman gratefully accepted Emilia's gift, but, when she went to take the bucket, Lucienne shrieked a warning to her not to touch it because Emilia had poisoned the snails. She then departed with her luggage in the car of a male friend, laughing all over her wicked face.

When Emilia returned, the washerwoman accused her of poisoning the snails, which, Emilia told me, certainly *had* been tampered with and had turned a bright green. Later it transpired that Lucienne herself had poured boiling water and *cristaux de soude* (a very acrid and burning variety of washing soda) upon them, not knowing of Emilia's gift to the washerwoman and evidently hoping that Emilia would poison herself and her family. Hilaire saw her do it, and, knowing nothing of either presentation, thought it was Madame's order.

We are not yet become quite civilised in Provence, it seems, and our passions are easily aroused.

But to return to our more pleasant harvests. Our figs we do not bother to pick in quantity, but just devour as many as we can until their season is over. Even so, the ground is black with them, because they grow in such profusion everywhere that they are unsaleable and allowed by the Provençaux to drop off the trees and rot. Those who like dried figs collect their surplus and lay them out upon wire frames (on legs) to dry in the sun ; but having seen the masses of flies that settle upon them during this drying process, I could never touch them.

Once upon a time figs were so popular that every peasant grew them for export, but now the fashion has changed, and for many years the trees have been neglected. They produce hundreds of small sweet figs, but none of any size. Monsieur had a passion for them, and Hilaire, grinning with delight, used to bring him a plateful for his breakfast every morning, and every evening Monsieur himself gathered enough for dessert with the aid of the curious Provençal implement used for picking fruit, called a *cueille-fruit*. This is a tin funnel with a jagged pointed edge, placed on a long pole. You place it under your peach or fig, arranging that the twig to which the fruit is attached lies in one of the sharp V's of the jagged edge. An upward thrust and the twig is severed, and the fruit falls into the funnel and can be lowered to the ground. A primitive but very useful device. We have had great sport with our *cueille-fruit*, and I have even caught lizards in it and detached wasps' nests, which here hang like pretty little pointed bags on the eaves of buildings.

But the greatest excitement of all was our first grape harvest. Every peasant for miles around us was having his or her *vendange*, and everyone met was stained purple. There are four hundred and fifty vines fringing the terraces of the Domaine, a mixed variety of grapes and many choicer kinds, such as Black Hamburg and Muscats. Evidently the peasant who originally owned the little property had made up to the gardeners of neighbouring millionaire-estates and persuaded them to give him *greffes* to be grafted upon the wild vines.

At first we thought all our vines were ordinary ones, until one day I spied a gigantic cluster of translucent purple grapes and tasted one, expecting to be screwed up into a ball with its acrid flavour. Instead, I was delighted by something rare and precious, so I cut off the bunch and raced indoors with it to Monsieur, who pronounced it to be a *Cinsaut Noir* vine. Thenceforth we searched for other treasures along our terraces, and discovered at least forty vines bearing aristocratic grapes.

So when the moment comes to harvest the fruit, I rush forth and tie white linen flags to the choice vines to warn the pickers that these grapes must be left for the delectation of the inmates of the Domaine and its guests.

The moment summer begins and the sun is really hot, the vines grow in the terrifying Provençal manner (Jack's beanstalk, which sprang up to the heavens in one night, must have been planted in Provence), and then begins the labour of tying them up and of breaking off suckers from the too luxuriant growth. Of course, Madame is roped in to do this tiresome work, because her fingers are more deft than Hilaire's horny ones; but the after-care is his great interest and delight, and she has long since remarked that tending vines is Hilaire's favourite pastime—for a variety of reasons.

For instance, when attractive girl guests are staying at the Domaine, the vines provide an effective screen behind which Hilaire can hide opposite the bedroom windows of these fascinating ladies. The garden being terraced upon different levels, it is possible to peer right into the windows of certain rooms, and this, I regret to say, Hilaire does. Emilia warned me first of this habit of his, for she saw him standing on a stone stairway behind the vines, dodging and peeping into the windows in the very early morning to see if he could catch a glimpse of the *demoiselles Anglaises* lying in bed. Emilia illustrated her story with a lively pantomime of the antics of Hilaire, during which I found it extremely difficult to preserve a becomingly shocked expression. She ended her recital with the disgusted remark: " *Un homme de son age !* " (" A man of his age ! ")

I felt that the reproval of Hilaire upon such delicate matters should be left to Monsieur, who, however, rebuked him with such levity of mien and manner that he did more harm than good. Hilaire saw at once that irresistible twinkle in the eye of Monsieur, and any hope of making an impression upon him was lost for ever. True, he no longer stood openly upon that staircase, but I noticed that he invariably found work to do upon those terraces directly opposite the guest-rooms, and the other day I was obliged to tackle him myself.

He grinned sheepishly, tapped his old nose, and informed me that " *le pauvre Monsieur* " had once spoken to him about this, and then added : " *Madame a raison. Ce n'est pas joli ça* " (" Madame is right. It isn't pretty to do that.") But still he goes on doing it.

He confided to Emilia that the English ladies wore *robes du soir* (evening dresses) in bed. I suppose poor old sad-faced Madame Hilaire, who suffers from chronic rheumatism, wears high-necked, long-sleeved calico in summer and flannel in winter, hence his interest in the attire of my friends.

Many of the English in Provence make their own wine, but we have no wine-press, and in any case good matured wine is so cheap out here that it is hardly worth while for amateurs to attempt wine-making. So we sell our crop, and although, on good years when grapes are plentiful, the price works out at about one franc per kilo (over two pounds), we decided to keep our vines for the interest of their cultivation and the fun of the annual *vendange*, not to mention the sheer beauty of the vines and grapes as an edging to our terraces.

First, one gets the tender green leaves and tendrils, which look so lovely as the sun shines through them ; then the leaves are sprayed with sulphate of copper (to keep off disease), which leaves spots and stains of brilliant turquoise blue ; after that appear clusters of purple and golden grapes nestling among the thick screens of leaves ; and finally, when the grapes are all picked, those leaves turn yellow, bronze, crimson, and purple, giving a glory of colour.

We always beg our English neighbours to come and help us harvest our grapes. The first crop we harvested weighed over a ton, in spite of the fact that we missed out two complete terraces where the grapes were less fine, everyone rushing to the most prolific vines to cut the largest bunches. The busiest harvester was ' George,' a large bull-terrier, who tore off large bunches with his teeth and devoured the grapes hungrily until discovered by his mistress and leashed reluctantly to an olive-tree. I knew that little foxes spoiled grapes, but until then I had no idea that dogs did.

At the end of the day Emilia appeared with lemon juice, syphons, and ice, and was greeted rapturously by the harvesters. The Domaine tee-total drinks gain a more piquant flavour through their presentation. For some reason only known to herself, Emilia gives each drinker his or her ration of fruit juice in a different vessel. They are all a part of the same Celadon green service ; but I have seen a guest's eyebrow shoot up involuntarily, a twinkle in an eye, or a twist at the corner of a sedate mouth as Emilia presents one portion in an egg-cup, another in a cream-jug, and a really thirsty person with a sugar-basin. We have plenty of crystal jugs and glasses, but these are left in their cupboard. I have never corrected this queer little habit, for it amuses me and reminds me of our early days in Provence before Emilia learned the uses of porcelain, glass, and silver, and of that happy evening when she presented Monsieur and me with a delicious dish of *gnocchi* served up in the curved tin basin of the English weighing-scales. When Emilia has become perfectly sophisticated she will be far less of a joy.

Monsieur always adored his *vendange*, and worked indefatigably. I shall always have a happy vision of him running down a stone stairway with his arms full of grapes, a big bunch in his mouth, and his eyes dancing.

Last year, on the day fixed for our *vendange*, it poured tropically with rain. I telephoned to the peasant proprietor who had bought our crop and asked him if he would prefer it picked on another day when the fruit was dry, as I feared the wet grapes would ferment unless made at once into wine. He replied that he wanted to mix our fruit with his own, which he had picked at dawn (before the rain began), so that he could make his wine that evening. There was nothing for it but to brave the downpour, and if there is any wetter pursuit than picking grapes in rain I should be interested to know what it is.

Some of us wore bathing-suits, others were clad in ancient skirts, sou'-westers, and oil-skins. One courageous girl wore an old jumper and skirt and no hat. Her wet laughing face, framed in lank wisps of hair, occasionally poked through the dripping screens of leaves as she saluted another drowned rat on a lower terrace. The only creature who really enjoyed the weather was ' Charlotte,' a tame duck who accompanied her owner.

We were soaked to the skin ; water squelched out of our sand-shoes and *espadrilles* with a sucking squelching sound. Monsieur, having been ill, was forbidden by his tiny nurse to join the harvesters, to his grief and anger. At one moment he broke bounds, and just as I was explaining to my neighbour that we dared not let him help pick grapes she hissed in my ear, " 'Ware, Monsieur ! " and there he was behind me. It was very painful to resist those pleading eyes and to send him indoors again, but it had to be done. We consoled him a little, however, by suggesting

Weighing the grapes.

that he should sit in the covered porch and superintend the weighing of his crop at the end of the day when the *camion* (lorry) came to collect it.

A picturesque affair is that weighing. Two sturdy peasants stand about twelve feet apart with a large pole placed on their shoulders. The grapes are put into oblong wooden cases (which have been previously weighed), and these cases are slung in turn upon the pole with a balance between them. The weight is then called out to an umpire, who records it in a notebook.

The crop very nearly did not reach its destination. It was duly weighed and the cases packed into the *camion*, which got safely down the drive and out of the gate of the Domaine. But at the first dangerous bend in the mountain track it met a celebrated mule dragging a cart laden with sacks of coke. It so happened that the muleteer, whom the mule knew and loved, had been obliged to leave his work to go up into the mountains to visit a sick daughter, and the mule had been left in the charge of a raw youth whose one idea was to save himself trouble. Instead of halving the load of coke and bringing it in two journeys to save the mule, he had rashly piled all the sacks on the cart. The mule was already furiously indignant when he encountered the *camion*, which gave him an excellent excuse to stop dead and then begin to play hell. He rose up on his hind-legs and did a clumsy *pas-seul;* he then bucked energetically, and suddenly started backing at a tremendous speed towards the precipitous edge of the road just above the terraces of my neighbour the Corsican brigand. The boy in charge seized the bridle, but was swung high up into the air as the mule reared finally before backing the cart and boy over the edge of the void and disappearing with them. The animal turned a complete somersault; the boy turned several as he rolled down the mountain; the cart was smashed to atoms, and the sacks of coke rolled in an avalanche down over six terraces into the garden of the fortunate Corsican brigand below. The mule was slightly scratched, the boy unhurt; and the Corsican and his family were supplied with fuel free of charge for the whole winter, for the hour was late and it was impossible to gather up all the spilt coke before it was dark, and such a gift, falling literally from the heavens, was not likely to be ignored by poor grateful peasants.

In spite of the rain, the whole neighbourhood, including, of course, my Hilaire, rushed to the scene of the disaster to disentangle the mule from the branches of an olive-tree and to revive the terrified boy. The cart was merely a mass of splinters, which also doubtless proved very useful firewood for my neighbour, who did not even have the trouble of cutting it up. The wonder was that neither the mule nor his inconsiderate driver fell into the great irrigation tank on those dangerous terraces.

In the meanwhile our harvest of grapes had

to sit in the *camion*, washed over by torrential rain, until the mountain track was clear of mules, coke, boys, and helpful neighbours, for at that particular point it is impossible for any vehicles to pass each other.

The wine-makers must have worked all night to make their vintage, and perhaps that was why we got so miserable a price for our grapes.

The *vendange* of Emilia's brother also took place at night. She asked for leave to go to his house to help him make his wine, and afterwards described the scene to me. He had been working at his job (he is a mason) all day, and so not until evening could he attend to the crushing of his grapes. Then he and his complete family—wife, children, sisters, brothers, and cousins—assembled in a huge vaulted cellar under a crooked archway. Torches were lighted and stuck into crevices in the walls, and everyone, even his lovely little daughter of five years old, crowned with vine-leaves and a bunch of grapes hanging over each ear, helped to carry armfuls of grapes to the square crushing machine placed over a great tub, while Emilia and her brother turned the wheel.

One can imagine the chattering that went on and how hot they all got, and picture the scene as the torchlight flickered over those glistening grape-stained faces and shone in their dark eyes.

We were fortunate in that our little domaine proves to have the richest soil in the province, and that everything we plant grows and prospers. We chose this particular spot, half-way down one mountain and sheltered by the great shoulder of another, because of its beauty and amenities, then knowing nothing of soils and devastating winds, so that we had all the joys of discovery.

A chauffeur gave me a bunch of carnations for New Year, and, as an experiment, I pulled the side-whiskers off the stalks and stuck them in the ground with hope and love, but with very little faith that they would grow. Now I have a flourishing plot of sturdy carnations which bloom continuously from May to July, or even later if I conscientiously cut off the dead blooms.

Stray peach, plum, and apricot stones, spat forth carelessly in the garden by guests, take root and prosper; and this year there has been no necessity to plant annuals in the flower-beds because the flowers of last year seeded themselves so generously that very soon I shall have a lovely display.

Since we took possession of the little domaine, Hilaire, Monsieur, and I have planted and watered frantically, but God certainly does give the increase,—perhaps partly through the kindly intercession of our Bishop.

I happened to be sitting next to him at a luncheon-party soon after the enlargement of our little house was finished, and I asked him if I might ask him a 'shoppy' question. He twinkled at me encouragingly and begged me to speak. I told him that I had heard that every true Provençale invites the village priest to come and bless a new property, and I wondered if in our English Church we ever did the same, as, if we did not, I intended to ask the village *curé* to do it for I wanted my house blest.

The Bishop replied : " I can assure you that we do it quite as efficiently as the Roman Catholics. I, myself, will come up and bless your little domaine to-morrow evening."

His kindness confused me, for, when I asked my question, I never dreamed that he would propose coming himself.

He came at sunset next day. Not having expected that such a service might be required of him during his visit to the Riviera, he had brought no form of printed prayer from England ; and so he asked me first to take him all over the house and to tell him for what purpose each room was used. He then put on his full vestments, took his crozier in his hand, and preceded Monsieur and me from room to room, blessing each in turn in his own simple appropriate words. In every room he prayed for the blessing of peace.

It was a quiet, homely little ceremony, and when we went out into the garden, there was old Hilaire tending his vines in the distance, and the two little maids hanging out the family washing down in the olive grove. I dreamily noted a goodly crop of familiar garments, among them the blue *caleçons* of Monsieur, Emilia's mauve overall, and my own apricot night-dress, proudly displayed upon the line for all the world to see.

The Bishop took his stand upon the steps of the rose-garden, the sunset light shining upon his mitre and vestments as he blessed the glory of flowers around us and prayed that our vines and fruit-trees might prosper and bring forth abundance.

Hilaire bared his old bald head respectfully, and the maids stood silently apart as, with an enveloping gesture, the Bishop blessed them too.

Finally, he led Monsieur and me back into our little hall and made us both kneel while he blessed us both, praying that in spite of all worldly struggles and trials we might be given the peace that passes all understanding.

And this prayer was answered, for when after

a gallant fight in hospital the beloved Monsieur was taken from me, he did, after all, have perfect peace at the last, for he fell asleep like a tired child, thinking that he was in his own little domaine and never knew that he was leaving me alone.

Winifred Fortescue was born in a Suffolk rectory on 7th February, 1888, the third child of a country rector and connected, on her mother's side, to the Fighting Battyes of India.

When she was seventeen – in order to ease the strain on family finances – she decided to try to earn her own living, and went on the stage, performing in Sir Herbert Tree's company, and later starring in Jerome J. Jerome's *The Passing of the Third Floor Back*.

In 1914 she married John Fortescue, the King's Librarian and Archivist and famous historian of the British Army. The marriage, in spite of a huge disparity of age between them, was a uniquely happy one, and although Winifred Fortescue gave up her career on the stage, she later began a successful interior decorating and dress designing business until illness forced her to close her company down. It was at that point that she began writing, for *Punch*, the *Daily Chronicle*, the *Evening News*, finally inaugurating and editing a Woman's Page for the *Morning Post*.

In the early 1930s, John and Winifred Fortescue, now Sir John and Lady Fortescue, moved to Provence and there she wrote her famous and bestselling *Perfume From Provence*. She died at Opio, Provence, in April 1951.